D1073691

Love for the Papacy

*and Filial Resistance to the Pope
in the History of the Church*

ROBERTO DE MATTEI

Love for the Papacy
&
Filial Resistance to the Pope
in the
History of the Church

✝

Foreword by
Raymond Leo Cardinal Burke

 Angelico Press

First published in the USA
by Angelico Press 2019
© Roberto de Mattei 2019
Foreword © Raymond Leo Cardinal Burke 2019

For information, address:
Angelico Press
169 Monitor St.
Brooklyn, NY 11222
www.angelicopress.com

ISBN 978 1 62138 455 7 pb
ISBN 978 1 62138 456 4 cloth
ISBN 978 1 62138 457 1 ebook

Cover design: Michael Schrauzer

CONTENTS

PART II: LECTURES

Foreword

AT A TIME OF profoundest spiritual and moral crisis, the Catholic Church needs more than ever before to recall her Sacred Tradition, unbroken from the time of the Apostles. Only by fidelity to Sacred Tradition can the Bride of Christ, amid the many challenges she faces, chart her course, in accord with the will of Christ, her Bridegroom, her Head and Shepherd at every time and in every place.

With his wealth of historical knowledge and his perspective firmly grounded in the "deposit of faith," Professor Roberto de Mattei makes an invaluable contribution to the life of the Church in our time. Not only is he keenly aware of the crises that Christ has overcome in His Mystical Body all along the Christian centuries, he is supremely confident that the future of the Church is one in which the victory of Christ is assured through the intercession of the Immaculate Heart of Mary. Thus, Professor de Mattei helps the Christian faithful, as cooperators with the divine grace that flows immeasurably and unceasingly from the glorious pierced Heart of Christ into their hearts, to remain faithful in His cause, giving an account of their faith to the world today and defending the faith from the many attacks that it suffers daily.

May these reflections inspire and bless many of the Christian faithful as they strive to live the Truth of Jesus Christ in His Love, guided by the Holy Spirit, as sons and daughters of the One, Holy, Catholic, and Apostolic Church.

RAYMOND LEO CARDINAL BURKE
April 22, 2019, Monday of Easter Week

Preface

THE PURPOSE of this book, which contains several of my articles and conference presentations from the last few years, is to contribute to an understanding of the grave crisis of the contemporary Church. In order to understand the nature and cause of this crisis, theology and philosophy are certainly necessary, because, as Donoso Cortés affirms, every question has a religious and metaphysical root. And yet without the assistance of history it is difficult to understand what the correct attitude of Catholics should be in the hour of trial. For this reason I often use historical examples, showing how they can help us to face situations that seem unprecedented and present no obvious way out.

The Gospel image of the boat tossed by the storm (Mt 8:23–27; Mk 4:35–41; Lk 8:22–25) was often used by the Fathers of the Church and the saints, who speak of the Church as a little boat pounded by the waves, enduring every storm, without ever allowing herself to be capsized. Trials and disturbances have accompanied the Church throughout her history, but the most terrible storms of all have come from within the Church herself. Saint Paul in his epistles often refers to the schisms and heresies that, already in his time, were appearing among the faithful. Thus, in the fourth chapter of his Letter to the Ephesians, he admonishes them to "no longer live as the Gentiles do, in the futility of their minds, darkened in understanding, alienated from the life of God because of their ignorance" (Eph 4:17–18). The origin of this alienation from the life of God lies in man's lack of submission to the saving doctrine of Jesus Christ, the one Way, Truth, and Life. This faith constitutes the foundation on which Jesus Christ built his Church and on which she remains firm until the end of time. When the storm raged and the boat was thrashed by the waves, the disciples drew close to the sleeping Jesus, and waking him they cried out: "Lord, save us! We are perishing!" And He said to them: "Why are you terrified, O you of little faith?" Then he got up, rebuked the winds and the sea, and there was great calm. The men were amazed, and said, "What sort of man is this, whom even the winds and the sea obey?" (Mt 23:27).

Only Jesus Christ can save the Church—no one else— because He alone is her Founder and Head. Human beings, from the Vicar of Christ down to the last member of the faithful, can either cooperate with or resist the divine grace that comes to them through the influence of the Holy Spirit and impels them to radical fidelity to Christ and His Law.

In times of trial, it is not we who can save the Church. We can only serve her and love her more deeply, imitating the example of those who, over the course of history, have given their lives for her. So also these essays have been written with the sole intention of serving and loving the Church.

Most of the translations in this volume were prepared by Francesca Romana, the pen name of a frequent contributor to the website Rorate Caeli. They were subsequently edited for this volume.

Roberto de Mattei
February 28, 2019

PART I

ESSAYS

The Spirit of Resistance and Love for the Church[1]

MORE THAN six years into Pope Francis's pontificate, we hear repeatedly that we are facing a dramatic and absolutely unprecedented page in the story of the Church. This is only partly true. The Church has always experienced tragic times that have seen the laceration of the Mystical Body, from its very beginnings on Calvary right up to the present day.

The younger generations do not know and the older generations have forgotten how terrible were the years that followed the Second Vatican Council, of which the present age is the result. Fifty years ago, while the 1968 revolt was erupting, a group of cardinals and bishops who were protagonists at the council sought to impose a radical change on the Catholic doctrine of marriage. The attempt was frustrated by way of Paul VI's encyclical *Humanae Vitae* of July 25, 1968, which reaffirmed the prohibition of artificial contraception, restoring strength and hope to a disorientated flock. However, the Paul VI of *Humanae Vitae* was also the one who caused a deep rupture with Catholic Tradition in 1969 by imposing the new rite of the Mass, which is at the origin of all contemporary liturgical devastation.

On November 18, 1973, the same pope promoted *Ostpolitik* by assuming the grave responsibility of removing Cardinal József Mindszenty (1892–1975) from his office as

1. Originally published in *Corrispondenza Romana* on February 7, 2018. This and other essays translated by Francesca Romana.

Archbishop of Esztergom, Primate of Hungary—and champion of Catholic opposition to Communism. Pope Montini had hoped for the attainment of a historical compromise in Italy, based on the alliance between the Secretary of the Christian Democrats, Aldo Moro, and the Secretary of the Communist Party, Enrico Berlinguer. The operation was abruptly interrupted by the kidnapping and killing of Moro in 1978, after which Pope Montini himself died the following August 6.

During those years of betrayal and blood, courageous voices spoke out, which we of necessity recall, not simply for the record, but because they help us to orient ourselves in the darkness of the present time. We remember two, prior to the explosion of the so-called "Lefebvre Case," which Bishop Athanasius Schneider highlighted in a recent interview on his "prophetic mission during an extraordinarily dark time of general crisis in the Church."[2]

The first voice belongs to a French Dominican priest, Father Roger Calmel (1914–1975), who right from the very beginning in 1969 had rejected Paul VI's *Novus Ordo* and in June 1971 wrote in the magazine *Itinéraires* the following:

> Our Christian resistance of priests and laity [is] very painful resistance as it forces us to say no to the pope himself about the modernist manifestation of the Catholic Mass; our respectful but unshakable resistance is dictated by the principle of total fidelity to the living Church of all time; or, in other words, from the principle of living fidelity to the development of the Church. Never have we thought of holding back, or even less of impeding, what some, with very ambiguous words, for that matter, call "progress" in the Church; we'd call it rather the homogeneous growth in doctrinal and liturgical matters, in continuation with Tradition, in sight of the *consummatio sanctorum*. As Our

2. Interview with Edward Pentin, published online in the *National Catholic Register*, January 11, 2018.

Lord has revealed to us in parables, and as St. Paul teaches us in his Epistles, we believe that the Church, over the course of the centuries, grows and develops in harmony through a thousand adversities, until the glorious return of Jesus Himself, her Spouse and our Lord. Since we are convinced that over the course of centuries a growth of the Church is occurring, and since we are resolute in our desire to become part of this mysterious and uninterrupted movement as integrally as possible, as far as it is up to us, we reject this supposed progress which refers to Vatican II and which in reality is mortal deviation. Going back to St. Vincent of Lérin's classical distinction, the more we desire good growth—a splendid *profectus*—the more do we reject, uncompromisingly, a ruinous *permutatio* and any radical and shameful alteration whatsoever; radical, since it comes from modernism and denies all faith; shameful, since the denial of the modernist sort is shifty and hidden.

The second voice is that of a Brazilian thinker and man of action, Plinio Corrêa de Oliveira (1908–1995), author of a leaflet of resistance to the Vatican *Ostpolitik*, which appeared on April 10, 1974, published by Tradition, Family and Property, entitled *The Vatican Policy of Détente with Communist Governments—Should the TFPs Stand Down? Or Should they Resist?*

Corrêa de Oliveira explained: "To resist means that we would advise Catholics to continue fighting against the Communist doctrine through all legitimate means, in defense of Country and Christian civilization under threat." He added:

The lines of this declaration would not be sufficient to contain the list of all the Fathers of the Church, Doctors, moralists and canon lawyers—many of whom have been beatified or canonized—who sustain the legitimacy of resistance. A resistance that is not separation, nor revolt, nor acrimony, nor irreverence. On the contrary it is fidelity, union, love and submission. "Resistance" is the word we have chosen on purpose, as it has been used by St. Paul himself to describe his stance. Since the first pope, St. Peter, had taken disciplinary measures to retain practices in the Catholic Faith that survived the ancient Synagogue, St. Paul saw in this a grave risk of doctrinal confusion and harm for the faithful. So he rose up and "resisted" St. Peter "to his face" who did not see an act of rebellion in this energetic and inspired action by the Apostle to the Gentiles, but [an act] of union and fraternal love. Furthermore, knowing well where he was infallible and where he wasn't, he yielded to St. Paul's arguments. The saints are model Catholics. In the sense that St. Paul resisted, our position is resistance. In this, our conscience finds peace.

"Resistance" is not a purely verbal declaration of faith but an act of love towards the Church, an act that leads to practical consequences. Those who resist are separated from the one who has caused the division in the Church; they criticize him openly; they correct him. In 2017, they expressed themselves along these lines with the *Correctio filialis* to Pope Francis, and the *Fidelity Pledge* of pro-life leaders appeared with the title: "Faithful to true doctrine, not to pastors who are in error."[3]

Today, a similar manifestation may be seen in Cardinal Joseph Zen's stance of no compromise in regard to Pope Francis's new *Ostpolitik* towards Communist China. To those who object that it is necessary "to try to find common ground to bridge the decades-old division between the Vatican and China," Cardinal Zen replies: "But can there ever be anything 'in common' with a totalitarian regime? Either you surrender or you accept persecution, but remain faithful to yourself. (Can you imagine an agreement between St. Joseph and Herod?)" To those who ask him whether he is convinced that the Vatican is selling out the Catholic Church in China,

3. See https://www.fidelitypledge.com/.

he says: "Decidedly, yes. If they are going in the direction that is obvious in everything they have done in recent months and years."[4]

On April 7, 2018, a conference took place on the present crisis in the Church, with the participation of some cardinals and bishops, and above all, Cardinal Zen. From the meeting a voice was raised, full of love for the Church and firm resistance to all the theological, moral, and liturgical deviations of the present pontificate—but without insinuating the invalidity of Benedict XVI's abdication or Pope Francis's election. Taking refuge in a canonical problem means avoiding debate of the doctrinal problem, which is at the root of the crisis we are experiencing.

4. Cardinal Joseph Zen, statement on his Facebook page, January 28, 2018.

The Irrevocable Duties of Cardinals of the Holy Roman Church[1]

I N HIS ADDRESS given at the Lepanto Foundation on December 5, 2016, Cardinal Raymond Burke said:

> There is a very heavy burden on a cardinal's shoulders. We are the pope's Senate and his primary counselors and must, above all, serve the pope, by telling him the truth. Submitting questions, as we have done to the pope, is in the Church's tradition, specifically to avoid divisions and confusion. We did this with the highest respect for the Petrine Office, without lacking reverence to the person of the pope. There are many questions, but the five main questions we have posed must, of necessity, have a response for the salvation of souls. We pray every day for a response, faithful to Tradition, in the uninterrupted apostolic line that takes us back to Our Lord Jesus Christ.[2]

With these words Cardinal Burke brought to mind the importance of the mission of cardinals, the highest in the Catholic Church after that of the Supreme Pontiff. They are in fact the pope's foremost counsellors and collaborators in the governing of the Universal Church. Their institution is very ancient, seeing that already during the pontificate of Sylvester I (314–335) we find reference to the term *diaconi*

---

1. Originally published in *Corrispondenza Romana* on December 14, 2016.

2. Source: http://www.robertodemattei.it/en/2016/12/14/the-irrevocable -duties-of-cardinals-of-the-holy-roman-church/.

cardinales. It seems that we owe the definition of the Sacred College as "Senate of the Church," acknowledged by the 1917 Code of Canon Law (can. 230), to St. Peter Damian. The Sacred College of Cardinals has a juridical character that endows it with the triple nature of coadjutor body, substitute body, and electoral body of the Supreme Pontiff.

We must not commit the error of elevating the role of cardinals from being counsellors to the pope to that of "co-decision-makers." Even if he leans on counsel and assistance from his cardinals, the pope never loses his *plenitudo potestatis*. The cardinals participate in the power of the pope only within the limits defined by the Pontiff himself. The cardinals never have deliberative powers in their relation to the pope but only advisory ones. If the pontiff should avail himself of assistance from the College of Cardinals even if he is not obliged to do so, for their part, the cardinals have the moral duty to counsel the Pontiff, submit questions to him, and admonish him, independent of the pope's reception of their words. The presentation by the four cardinals (Brandmüller, Burke, Caffarra, and Meisner) of certain *dubia* to the pope and Cardinal Müller, Prefect of the Congregation for the Doctrine of the Faith, asking them to clarify "the grave disorientation and great confusion" relating to the Apostolic Exhortation *Amoris Laetitia*, enters perfectly within the duties of cardinals and cannot be the object of any censure.

As the canonist Edward Peters, referendary to the Supreme Tribunal of the Apostolic Signatura, affirmed, the four cardinals "[made] text-book use of their rights under Canon 212 §3 to pose doctrinal and disciplinary questions that urgently need addressing in our day."[3] If the Holy Father should omit answering these questions, the cardinals collectively will address him with a form of fraternal correc-

---

3. Source: https://canonlawblog.wordpress.com/2016/11/29/cardinals-in -the-church-have-rights-too/.

tion, in the spirit of admonition made by St. Paul to the Apostle Peter at Antioch (Gal 2:11).

The canonist affirmed:

> How anyone can conclude, then, based on the facts at hand, that the four cardinals are at risk for deprivation of their office, escapes me. No one, least of all the four cardinals in question, challenges the special authority that a pope enjoys over the Church (1983 CIC 331) nor do they harbor any illusions that a pope could be forced to answer the questions they posed. My hunch is that the four cardinals, while they would welcome a papal reply, are probably content with having formally preserved these vital questions for a day when a direct answer might be forthcoming—although they might yet exercise their own episcopal office as teachers of the faith (1983 CIC 375) and propose answers on their own authority. For that, these men are, I think, prepared to accept personal ridicule and to suffer misunderstanding and misrepresentation of their actions and motives.

The dignity of a cardinal is not purely honorary, but involves grave responsibilities. Cardinals have privileges because first of all they have duties. The honors given to them derive precisely from the burden of responsibilities that weighs on their shoulders. Among these responsibilities there is that of fraternally correcting the pope when he commits an error in the governing of the Church, as happened in 1813, when Pius VII signed the ill-fated Treaty of Fontainebleau with Napoleon, or in 1934 when the Dean of the College of Cardinals, Gennaro Granito di Belmonte (1851–1948), admonished Pius XI on behalf of the Sacred College for the rash use he made of the Holy See's finances. The pope is infallible only under determined circumstances, and his acts of government or Magisterium can contain errors that any one of the faithful may point out, with even greater reason if the latter is invested with the office of principal counselor to the Supreme Pontiff.

The Irrevocable Duties of Cardinals

Among the medieval canonists who dealt with the College of Cardinals, one who excels is Enrico da Susa, also called Ostiense (since he was the Cardinal Bishop of Ostia), an author who was the object of a recent study by Don Jürgen Jamin.[4] Professor Jamin recalls that Enrico da Susa, while commenting on the Pontifical Decrees, considered the hypothesis of a pope who falls into heresy. He observes in particular Ostiense's comment on these words relating to the pope: "*Nec deficiat fides eius* [Nor may his faith be lacking]." According to the Cardinal Bishop of Ostia, "The faith of Peter is not exclusively his 'faith' meant as a personal act, but is the faith of the entire Church of which he is the spokesman and the Prince of the Apostles. Christ prays, therefore, for the faith of the entire Church *in persona tantum Petri* [in the person of Peter only], since it is the faith of the Church, professed by Peter, which never fails *et propterea ecclesia non presumitur posse errare* [and on this account the Church is not able to err]."[5]

Ostiense's thought matches that of all the great medieval canonists. The greatest modern scholar of these authors, Cardinal Alfonso Maria Stickler, points out that

> the prerogative of infallibility of office does not impede the pope, as an individual, from sin and thus from becoming personally heretical. . . . In the case of an obstinate and public profession of certain heresy, since it is condemned by the Church, the pope becomes *minor quolibet catholico* [lesser than any Catholic, a common phrase of canonists] and ceases to be pope. . . . This fact of a heretic pope does not touch then pontifical infallibility, since it does not signify impeccability or inerrancy in the person of the Pontiff, [or] inerrancy in establishing forcefully from his office

---

4. Don Jürgen Jamin, *The Cooperation of Cardinals in Pontifical Decisions,* ratione fidei: *The Thought of Enrico da Susa (Ostiene)* (Marcianum Press, Venice 2015).

5. Ibid., 223.

a truth of the faith or an immutable principle of Christian life.... The canonists knew very well how to distinguish between the person of the pope and his office. If then they declared the pope dethroned, when certainly and obstinately heretical, they admit implicitly that from this personal fact not only is the infallibility of the office not compromised, but that it is somewhat defended and affirmed: any "papal" decision whatever against a truth already decided is automatically rendered impossible.[6]

The cardinals who elect the pope do not have the authority to depose him, but may ascertain his renunciation of the pontificate, in the case of voluntary resignation or of manifest and persistent heresy. In the tragic times of history, they must serve the Church, even to the shedding of blood, as the color red indicates in the garments they wear and the formula at the imposition of the biretta states: "red as sign of the dignity of the cardinalate, signifying that you must be ready to act with fortitude, even unto the shedding of blood, for the increase in the Christian Faith, for the peace and tranquility of the people of God, and for the freedom and diffusion of Holy Mother Church."

For this we join the prayers of Cardinal Burke in asking Pope Francis to respond to the *dubia* in a manner "faithful to Tradition, in the uninterrupted Apostolic line which takes us back to Our Lord Jesus Christ."

---

6. Alfons M. Stickler, *Sulle origini dell'infallibilità papale*, in *Rivista Storica della Chiesa in Italia*, 28 (1974), 586–87.

When Public Correction
of a Pope is Urgent
and Necessary[1]

MAY A POPE be publicly corrected for his reprehensible behavior? Or should the attitude of the faithful be that of unconditional obedience to the point of justifying anything the pope says and does, even if openly scandalous?

According to some, like the Vatican journalist Andrea Tornielli, it is possible to express *tête-à-tête* one's dissent from the pope, without, however, manifesting it publicly. This thesis, nonetheless, implies an important admission. The pope is not infallible unless he speaks *ex cathedra*. Otherwise it would not be licit to dissent even privately, and the path to follow would only be that of religious silence. On the other hand, the pope, who is not Christ but only His representative on earth, can sin and make mistakes. Yet, is it true that he may only be corrected privately and never publicly?

To respond, it is important to recall the historical example *par excellence*, the so-called "incident at Antioch." St. Paul records it in these terms in his Epistle to the Galatians, probably written between A.D. 54 and 57:

> When they saw that I had been entrusted with the gospel
> to the uncircumcised, just as Peter to the circumcised,
> for the one who worked in Peter for an apostolate to the

---

1. Originally published in *Corrispondenza Romana* on February 22, 2017.

circumcised worked also in me for the Gentiles, and when they recognized the grace bestowed upon me, James and Cephas and John, who were reputed to be pillars, gave me and Barnabas their right hands in partnership, that we should go to the Gentiles and they to the circumcised. Only, we were to be mindful of the poor, which is the very thing I was eager to do. And when Cephas came to Antioch, I opposed him to his face because he clearly was wrong. For, until some people came from James, he used to eat with the Gentiles; but when they came, he began to draw back and separated himself, because he was afraid of the circumcised. And the rest of the Jews [also] acted hypocritically along with him, with the result that even Barnabas was carried away by their hypocrisy. But when I saw that they were not on the right road in line with the truth of the gospel, I said to Cephas in front of all, "If you, though a Jew, are living like a Gentile and not like a Jew, how can you compel the Gentiles to live like Jews?"

For fear of hurting the feelings of the Jews, Peter in his behavior favored the position of the "Judaizers," who believed that circumcision, along with other dispositions from the Mosaic law, should apply to all converted Christians. St. Paul says that St. Peter had been clearly wrong and therefore "he had withstood him to his face," that is, publicly, so that Peter would not be a scandal to the Church over which he exercised supreme authority. Peter accepted Paul's correction, acknowledging his error with humility.

St. Thomas Aquinas deals with this episode in several of his works. First of all, he notes that "the Apostle opposes Peter in his exercise of authority and not in his authority of government."[2] Paul recognized that Peter was the Head of the Church, but he judged it legitimate to resist him, given

2. *Super Epistolam ad Galatas lectura*, n. 77 (Edizioni Studio Domenicano, Bologna 2006).

the gravity of the problem, which concerned the salvation of souls. "The manner of the reprimand was appropriate as it was public and manifest."[3]

This episode, again notes the Angelic Doctor, contains as many teachings for prelates as for their subjects:

> To prelates [an example was given] of humility, so they would not refuse to accept complaints on the part of their inferiors and subjects; and to the subjects, examples of zeal and freedom so that they would not fear to correct their prelates, most of all when the fault was public and abounded in danger for many.[4]

At Antioch, St. Peter showed profound humility; St. Paul, ardent charity. The Apostle to the Gentiles showed that he was not only just but also merciful. Among the works of spiritual mercy there is the correction of sinners, called by moralists "fraternal correction." It is to be private if the sin is private and public if the sin is public. Jesus Himself established the manner:

> But if thy brother shall offend against thee, go, and rebuke him between thee and him alone. If he shall hear thee, thou shalt gain thy brother. And if he will not hear thee, take with thee one or two more: that in the mouth of two or three witnesses every word may stand. And if he will not hear them: tell the church. And if he will not hear the church, let him be to thee as the heathen and publican. Amen I say to you, whatsoever you shall bind upon earth, shall be bound also in heaven; and whatsoever you shall loose upon earth, shall be loosed also in heaven. (Mt 18:15–18)

We can imagine that after having tried to convince St. Peter privately, Paul did not hesitate in admonishing him publicly;

---

3. Ibid., n. 84.
4. Ibid., n. 77.

rather, says St. Thomas, "since St. Peter had sinned in front of everyone, he had to be reproached in front of everyone."[5]

Fraternal correction, as the theologians teach, is a non-optional precept; it is obligatory, above all for those who have offices of responsibility in the Church, since it derives from the natural law and positive divine law.[6] The admonishment can also be directed from inferiors to their superiors, and from the laity to prelates. To the question whether it is acceptable or even necessary to correct a superior publicly, St. Thomas in his *Commentary on the Sentences of Peter Lombard* responds in the affirmative, making note however of the need to act always with extreme respect. Therefore "prelates should not be corrected by their subjects in front of everyone, but humbly, in private, unless there is impending danger to the Faith; then in fact the prelate would become the lesser, if he had slipped into infidelity, and the subject would become the greater."[7]

The Angelic Doctor expresses himself in the same terms in the *Summa Theologiae*:

> If the Faith were endangered, a subject ought to rebuke his prelate even publicly. Hence Paul, who was Peter's subject, rebuked him in public, on account of the imminent danger of scandal concerning faith, and, as the gloss of Augustine says on *Galatians* 2:11, "Peter gave an example to superiors, that if at any time they should happen to stray from the straight path, they should not disdain to be reproved by their subjects."[8]

Cornelius a Lapide, summing up the thought of the Fathers and Doctors of the Church, writes:

5. *In IV Sententiarum*, Dist. 19, q. 2, a. 3 (Edizioni Studio Domenicano, Bologna 1999).

6. *Dictionnaire de Théologie Catholique* (Baader-Cistercians, Paris 1905), III:1908.

7. *In IV Sententiarum*, Dist. 19, q. 2, a. 2.

8. *Summa Theologiae*, IIa-IIae, q. 33, a. 4, ad 2.

Superiors may be corrected, with humility and charity by their inferiors, so that the Faith is defended; this is what is declared, on the basis of this passage, by St. Augustine, St. Cyprian, St. Gregory, St. Thomas and others cited above. They teach clearly that St. Peter, despite being superior, was corrected by St. Paul.... With good reason, therefore, St. Gregory said (*Homil.* 18 *in Ezech.*): "Peter was silent, so that, being the first in the apostolic hierarchy, he was also the first in humility." And St. Augustine affirmed (*Epist.* 19 *ad Hieronymum*): "by teaching that superiors must not refuse permission to their inferiors to correct them, St. Peter gave to posterity a most exceptional and holy example in being corrected by St. Paul, teaching that, in defence of the truth, and in charity, to the lesser are given the boldness of withstanding without fear against those greater than they."[9]

Fraternal correction is an act of charity. One of the gravest sins against charity is schism, which is separation from the authority of the Church, her laws, uses, and customs. Even a pope can fall into schism if he divides the Church, as the theologian Suárez explains[10] and Cardinal Journet confirms.[11]

Confusion reigns in the Church today. Some courageous cardinals have announced an eventual public correction of Pope Bergoglio, whose initiatives are becoming more disturbing and divisive each day that passes. The fact that he has neglected to respond to the cardinals' *dubia* on Chapter 8 of the Exhortation *Amoris Laetitia* enables and favors heretical or near-heretical interpretations on the matter of Holy Communion for the divorced and remarried. The confusion encouraged thereby produces tensions and internal

9. *Ad Gal.* 2, II, in *Commentaria in Scripturam Sacram*, vol. 17 (Vivès, Paris 1876).

10. *De schismate*, in *Opera omnia*, vol. 12, 733–34 and 736–37.

11. *L'Eglise du Verbe Incarné* (Desclée, Bruges 1962), 1:596.

fights, or rather, a situation of religious contraposition that foreshadows schism. An act of public correction is thus rendered urgent and necessary.

The Religious War of
the Fourth Century and
of Our Times[1]

T HE CHURCH advances through history forever victorious, in accordance with the marvelous plans of
God. The first three centuries reached their peak
under the reign of Emperor Diocletian (284–305). All
appeared to be lost. Discouragement was a temptation for
many Christians, and among them there were those who lost
the Faith. But those who persevered had the immense joy,
not many years later, of seeing the Cross of Christ blazing on
the banners of Constantine at the Battle of Saxa Rubra (312).
This victory changed the course of history. The Milan-Nico-
media Edict of 313, granting liberty to Christians, overturned
Nero's *senatus consultum* [decree of the senate], which had
proclaimed Christianity a *superstitio illicita* [illicit supersti-
tion]. The public Christianization of society had its beginnings in a climate of enthusiasm and fervor for the Faith
within Roman society.

In 325, the Council of Nicaea would seem to mark the
doctrinal rebirth of the Church, with the condemnation of
Arius, who denied the divinity of the Word. At Nicaea,
thanks to the decisive role of the deacon Athanasius (295–
373), subsequently bishop of Alexandria, the doctrine of the
"consubstantiality" or unity of nature of the three persons of
the Most Holy Trinity was defined.

---

1. Originally published in *Corrispondenza Romana* on April 25, 2018.

In the years that followed, between the orthodox position and the Arian heretics a "third party" made its way in: that of the "Semi-Arians," in turn divided among themselves into various currents, which all acknowledged a certain analogy between the Father and the Son, but denied that the Son had been "begotten, not made, consubstantial [*homoousios*] with the Father," as was affirmed in the Nicene Creed. They replaced the word *homoousios* with the term *homoiousios*, which means "of similar substance."

The heretics—the Arians and the Semi-Arians—had understood that their success would be dependent on two factors: the first was that they remain inside the Church; the second, that they obtain the support of the political powers, hence of Constantine and afterwards his successors. And indeed it so happened: an unprecedented crisis inside the Church that lasted for more than sixty years.

Nobody has described it better than Cardinal Newman in his book *The Arians of the Fourth Century* (1833), wherein he presented all the doctrinal nuances of the question. An Italian scholar, Professor Claudio Pierantoni, has recently outlined an enlightening parallel between the Arian controversy and the present debate on the Apostolic Exhortation, *Amoris Laetitia*.[2] However, even in 1973, Monsignor Rudolf Graber (1903–1992), Bishop of Regensburg, when recalling the figure of St. Athanasius on the sixteenth centenary of his death compared the crisis of the fourth century to that following the Second Vatican Council.[3]

---

2. "The Arian crisis and the current controversy about *Amoris laetitia*: a parallel," AEMAET *Wissenschaftliche Zeitschrift für Philosophie und Theologie*, 5.2 (2016): 250–78, accessible at www.aemaet.de.

3. *Athanasius und die Kirche unserer Zeit: zu seinem 1600 Todestag* (Kral 1973); English trans. *Athanasius and the Church of Our Time* (Van Duren, Buckinghamshire 1974).

Athanasius was harshly persecuted even by his confreres for his fidelity to orthodoxy, and between 336 and 366 was five times forced to abandon the city in which he was bishop, thus spending long years in exile and in strenuous combat in defense of the Faith. Two assemblies of bishops, at Caesarea and Tyre (334–335), condemned him for rebellion and fanaticism. Further, in 341, while a council of fifty bishops in Rome had proclaimed Athanasius innocent, a council at Antioch, in which more than ninety bishops took part, ratified the acts of the synods of Caesarea and Tyre and named an Arian as bishop of Alexandria in the place of Athanasius.

The subsequent Council of Sardica in 343 ended with a schism: the Western Fathers declared the deposition of Athanasius illegal and reconfirmed the Council of Nicaea, while those from the East condemned not only Athanasius, but also Pope Julius I (afterwards canonized), who had supported him. The Council of Sirmium (351) sought a middle ground between Catholic orthodoxy and Arianism. At the Council of Arles (353), the fathers, including the legate representing Liberius, who had succeeded St. Julius I as pope, signed a new condemnation of Athanasius.

The bishops were forced to choose between the condemnation of Athanasius and exile. St. Paulinus, Bishop of Trier, was almost the only one to battle for the Nicene Creed and was exiled to Phrygia, where he died following mistreatment at the hands of the Arians. Two years later, at the Council of Milan (355), more than three hundred bishops of the West signed the condemnation of Athanasius, and another orthodox Father, St. Hilary of Poitiers, was banished to Phrygia for his intransigent fidelity to orthodoxy.

In 357, Pope Liberius, overcome by the sufferings of exile and at the insistence of his friends, but also driven by "a love for peace," signed the Semi-Arian formula of Sirmium and broke communion with St. Athanasius, declaring him separated from the Roman Church, for his use of the term "consubstantial," as is testified in four letters transmitted to us by St. Hilary.[4]

Under the pontificate of the same Liberius, the councils of Rimini (359) and Seleucia (359), which together constituted a "great council," representative of the West and the East, abandoned the Nicaean term "consubstantial" and established an equivocal "middle way" between the Arians and St. Athanasius. It seemed as if rampant heresy had conquered the Church.

The councils of Seleucia and Rimini are not numbered by the Church today among the eight ecumenical councils of antiquity: there were, nonetheless, as many as 560 bishops present, almost the totality of the bishops at that time, and these councils were defined as "ecumenical" by their contemporaries. It was then that St. Jerome remarked that "the whole world groaned and woke astounded to find itself Arian."[5]

What is important to underline is that the controversy was not over a doctrinal dispute among some theologians, nor a simple clash between bishops where the pope had to act as an arbiter. It was a religious war in which all Christians were involved, from the pope down to the least of the faithful. Nobody closed themselves up in a spiritual bunker; nobody stood looking out the window, a mute spectator of the drama. Everyone was down in the trenches fighting on one side of the battle lines.

It was not easy at that time to understand whether one's own bishop was orthodox or not, but the *sensus fidei* was the compass by which to orient oneself. Cardinal Walter Brandmüller, while speaking in Rome on April 7, 2018, recalled

---

4. Manlio Simonetti, *La crisi ariana del IV secolo* (Institutum Patristicum Augustinianum, Rome 1975), 235–36.

5. *Dialogus adversus Luciferianos*, n. 19, PL 23:171.

how "the 'sensus fidei' acts as a sort of spiritual immune system, through which the faithful instinctively recognize or reject any error. Upon this 'sensus fidei' rests then—apart from the divine promise—also the passive infallibility of the Church, or the certainty that the Church, in her totality, shall never be able to fall into heresy."[6]

St. Hilary writes that during the Arian crisis the ears of the faithful who interpreted in an orthodox sense the ambiguous affirmations of the Semi-Arian theologians were holier than the lips of the priests. The Christians who for three centuries had resisted emperors were now resisting their own shepherds, in some cases even the pope, guilty, if not of open heresy, at least of grave negligence.

In his book on Saint Athanasius, Monsignor Rudolf Graber refers to the words of Joseph von Görres (1776–1848) in his book *Athanasius* (1838), which, although written at the time of the arrest of the Archbishop of Cologne Clemens August in 1837, still have extraordinary resonance today:

> The earth is shaking under our feet. We can foresee with certainty that the Church will emerge unscathed from such ruin, but nobody can say or conjecture who and what will survive. We, then, in advising, in recommending and raising our hands, would like to impede the evil by showing its signs. Even the mules who carry the false prophets bristle, pull back, and with human language throw back the injustice in the face of those striking them; those who do not see the sword drawn [by God] which closes off the way to them. Work then while it is day, since at night nobody can. It serves nothing to wait: waiting has done nothing more than aggravate things.[7]

6. Address "On Consulting the Faithful in Matters of Doctrine," given at the Symposium "Catholic Church, Where Are You Heading?," available at https://www.lifesitenews.com/news/cardinal-brandmueller-talk.

7. *Sant'Atanasio e la Chiesa del nostro tempo* (Editrice Civiltà, Brescia 1974), 83–84; cf. n. 3.

There are times when a Catholic is obliged to choose between cowardice and heroism, between apostasy and holiness. This is what happened in the fourth century and it is what is happening even today.

Honorius I:
The Controversial Case
of a Heretic Pope[1]

T HE CASE OF Pope Honorius is one of the most contro-
versial in the history of the Church. As the Church
historian Émile Amann rightly notes in the large
entry he dedicates to the Question of Honorius in the *Dictionnaire de Théologie Catholique*, the problem needs to be
treated in an unbiased manner and with the serene impar-
tiality that history owes to past events.[2]

At the center of the pontificate of Pope Honorius, who
reigned from 625 to 638, was the question of Monothelitism,
the last of the great Christological heresies. In order to please
the Byzantine Emperor Heraclius, desirous of guaranteeing
religious peace inside his kingdom, the Patriarch of Constantinople, Sergius, sought to find a compromise between
Catholic orthodoxy, according to which in Jesus Christ there
are two natures in one person, and the Monophysite heresy,
which attributed to Christ one person only and one nature
only. The result of the compromise was a new heresy, Monothelitism, according to which the double nature of Christ
was moved in his action by one operation only and one will
only. This is semi-Monophysitism, but truth is integral or it
is not the truth, and a moderate heresy is always heresy. The

---

1. Originally published in *Corrispondenza Romana* on December 30,
2015.

2. *Dictionnaire de théologie catholique*, 7:96–132.

Patriarch of Jerusalem, Sophronius, was among those who intervened with the greatest vigor in denouncing the new doctrine, which rendered the humanity of Christ futile and led to the Monophysitism already condemned by the Council of Chalcedon (451).

Sergius wrote to Pope Honorius to ask "in future that no one be permitted to affirm the two operations in Christ Our God" and to receive his support against Sophronius. Honorius unfortunately assented to the request. In a letter to Sergius he affirmed that "the will of Our Lord Jesus Christ was one only [*unam voluntatem fatemur*]," on account of "the fact that our human nature was assumed by the Divinity," and he invited Sophronius to be silent. The correspondence between Sergius and Honorius is preserved in the acts of the sixth ecumenical council.[3]

Strengthened by the support of the pope, Heraclius published a doctrinal formulary in 638 called the *Ecthesis* ("Exposition"), wherein he presented the new theory of the one divine will as official doctrine. Monothelitism prevailed for over forty years in the Byzantine Empire. At that time the most vigorous defender of the Faith was the monk Maximus, known as the Confessor, who took part in a synod convoked at the Lateran (649) by Pope Martin (649–55) to condemn Monothelitism. Both the pope and Maximus were forced into exile. Maximus's tongue and right hand were cut off for his refusal to subscribe to the Monothelite doctrines. Sophronius, Maximus, and Martin are today venerated by the Church as saints for their indomitable resistance to the Monothelite heresy.

3. Mansi, *Sacrorum conciliorum nova et amplissima Collectio* (henceforth Mansi), 9:529–54, republished in Latin, Greek and French by Arthur Loth, *La cause d'Honorius. Documents originaux avec traduction, notes et conclusion* (Victor Palmé, Paris 1870) and in Greek and German by Georg Kreuzer, *Die Honoriusfrage im Mittelalter und in der Neuzeit* (Anton Hiersemann, Stuttgart 1975).

Honorius I: Controversial Case of a Heretic Pope

The Catholic Faith was finally restored by the third council of Constantinople, the sixth ecumenical council of the Church, which convened on November 7, 680, in the presence of Emperor Constantine IV and the representatives of the new pope, Agatho (678–681). The council condemned Monothelitism and imposed an anathema against all those who had promoted or favored this heresy and included Pope Honorius in this condemnation.

In the thirteenth session, held on March 28, 681, after having proclaimed their intention to excommunicate Sergius, Cyrus of Alexandria, Pyrrhus, Paul, and Peter, the council fathers, all the Patriarchs of Constantinople, and Bishop Theodore of Pharan, affirmed: "And in addition to these, we decide that Honorius also, who was pope of elder Rome, be with them cast out of the Holy Church of God, and be anathematized with them, because we have found by his letter to Sergius that he followed his opinion in all things, and confirmed his wicked dogmas."[4]

On August 9, 681, at the end of the sixteenth session, the anathema against all the heretics and supporters of the heresy, including Honorius, was renewed: "*Sergio haeretico a-nathema, Cyro haeretico anathema, Honorio haeretico anathema, Pyrro haeretico anathema.*"[5] In the dogmatic decree of the eighteenth session, on September 16, 681, it is said that

> since he who never rests and who from the very beginning was the inventor of malice, that by making use of the serpent, introduced poisonous death to human nature, as then, even now, has found the instruments suited to his will: we allude to Theodore, who was Bishop of Pharan; Sergius, Pyrrhus, Paul, and Peter, who were prelates of this imperial city; and also to Honorius, who was pope of elder

---

4. Mansi, 11:556.
5. Ibid., 622.

Rome; ... therefore the suited instruments being found, he did not cease, through these, to provoke scandals and errors in the Body of the Church; and with unheard-of expressions disseminated amidst the faithful people the heresy of the one will and one operation in two natures of a [Person] of the Holy Trinity, of Christ, our true God, in agreement with the insane false doctrine of the impious Apollinaris, Severus, and Themistius.[6]

The authentic copies of the conciliar acts, signed by 174 council fathers and the Emperor, were sent to the five patriarchal sees, with particular concern for their ratification by the Roman See. However, since Pope St. Agatho died on January 10, 681, the council acts, after more than 19 months of a *sede vacante*, were ratified by his successor Leo II (682–683). In the letter sent May 7, 683 to the Emperor Constantine IV, the pope wrote: "We anathematize the inventors of the new error, that is, Theodore, Bishop of Pharan, Sergius, Pyrrhus, Paul, and Peter, betrayers rather than leaders of the Church of Constantinople, and also Honorius, who did not attempt to sanctify this Apostolic Church with the teaching of apostolic tradition, but by profane treachery permitted its purity to be polluted."[7]

That same year, Pope Leo ordered that the council acts be translated into Latin, that they be signed by all the bishops of the West, and that these signatures be conserved at the tomb of St. Peter. As the eminent Jesuit historian Hartmann Grisar observes: "So was the universal acceptance of the sixth council in the West desired, and this, as far as is known, took place without any difficulty."[8]

The condemnation of Honorius was confirmed by Leo II's successors, as attests the *Liber Diurnus Romanorum Pontifi-*

---

6. Ibid., 636–37.
7. Ibid., 733.
8. *Analecta romana* (Desclée, Rome 1899), 406–7.

cum and the acts of the seventh (787) and eighth (869–870) ecumenical councils of the Church.[9]

Abbé Amann judges historically untenable the position of those, like Cardinal Baronius, who maintained that the acts of the council had been altered. The Roman legates were present at the council; it would be difficult to imagine that they could have been tricked or had misreported on such an important and delicate point as the condemnation for heresy of a Roman Pontiff. Referring then to those theologians like St. Robert Bellarmine who, in order to save the memory of Honorius, denied the presence of explicit errors in his letters, Amann underlines that they raised a greater problem than the one they claimed to resolve, i.e. the infallibility of the acts of a council presided over by a pope. If, in fact, Honorius did not fall into error, the popes and the council that condemned him were wrong.

The acts of the sixth ecumenical council, approved by the pope and received by the universal Church, have a much stronger defining significance than Honorius's letters to Sergius. In order to save infallibility it is better to admit the historical possibility of a heretic pope, than to shatter the dogmatic definitions and the anathemas of a council ratified by a Roman Pontiff. It is common doctrine that the condemnation of the writings of an author is infallible when the error is anathematized with the note of heresy, whereas the ordinary Magisterium of the Church is not always necessarily infallible.

During the First Vatican Council, the *Deputatio Fidei* or doctrinal commission confronted the problem by setting out a series of rules of a general character, which may be applied not only in the case of Honorius but in all problems past or future that may be presented. It is not enough for the pope

9. C. J. Hefele, *Histoire des Conciles* (Letouzey et Ané, Paris 1909), 3:520–21.

to pronounce on a question of faith or morals regarding the universal Church; it is necessary that the decree of the Roman Pontiff is conceived in such a manner as to appear as a solemn and definitive judgment, with the intention of obliging all the faithful to believe.[10] There are, therefore, acts of the ordinary papal Magisterium that are non-infallible because they are devoid of the necessary defining character.

Pope Honorius's letters are devoid of these characteristics. They are undoubtedly magisterial acts, but in the non-infallible ordinary Magisterium there may be errors and even, in exceptional cases, heretical formulations. The pope can fall into heresy, but cannot ever pronounce a heresy *ex cathedra*. In Honorius's case, as the Benedictine patrologist Dom John Chapman observes, it cannot be affirmed that he intended to formulate a sentence *ex cathedra*, defining and binding: "Honorius was fallible, was wrong, was a heretic, precisely because he did not, as he should have done, declare authoritatively the Petrine tradition of the Roman Church."[11] His letters to Sergius, even if they were about the Faith, did not promulgate any anathema and do not correspond to the conditions required by the dogma of infallibility. Promulgated by the First Vatican Council, the principle of infallibility is saved, contrary to what the Protestants and the Gallicans thought. Further, if Honorius was anathematized, as Pope Hadrian II explained in the Roman Synod of 869, "the reason is that Honorius was accused of heresy, the only cause for which it is licit to inferiors to resist their superiors and to repel their perverse sentiments."[12]

Specifically based on these words, after having examined the case of Pope Honorius, the great Dominican theologian

10. Mansi, 52:1204–32.

11. *The Condemnation of Pope Honorius* (1907; reprint: Forgotten Books, London 2013), 110.

12. Mansi, 16:126.

Melchior Cano (1509–1560) sums up the safest doctrine in these terms: "It must not be denied that the Supreme Pontiff can be a heretic, of which one or two examples may be offered. However, that [a pope] in judgments on the faith has defined something against the faith, not even one [example] can be demonstrated."[13]

13. *De Locis Theologicis* 1 (Biblioteca de Autores Cristianos, Madrid 2006), vol. VI, 409.

St. Theodore the Studite and the "Synod of Adultery"[1]

THE "SYNOD OF ADULTERY," a ninth-century assembly of bishops, made history when it wanted to approve the praxis of a second marriage after the repudiation of a legitimate wife. St. Theodore the Studite (759–826) was the one who opposed it the most vigorously and for this was persecuted, imprisoned, and exiled, the latter three times.

It all started in January 795, when the Roman Emperor of the East (*Basileos*) Constantine VI (771–797) had his wife Maria of Armenia locked up in a monastery and began an illicit union with Theodora, the lady-in-waiting to his mother, Irene. A few months later the Emperor had her proclaimed "Augusta" Theodora, but being unable to convince the Patriarch Tarasios (730–806) to celebrate the new wedding, he finally found a minister willing to do so in the priest Joseph, *hegumen* (head) of the Monastery of Kathara on the Island of Ithaca, who officially blessed the adulterous union.

St. Theodore, born in Constantinople in 759, was at that time a monk in the Monastery of Saccudium in Bithynia, where his uncle Plato, who was also later venerated as a saint, was the abbot. Theodore reports that the unjust divorce produced great perturbation in the entire Christian population—*concussus est mundus* [the world has been

---

1. Originally published in *Corrispondenza Romana* on August 26, 2015.

shaken][2]—and along with St. Plato protested energetically, in the name of the indissolubility of the marriage bond. He wrote, "The Emperor must consider himself an adulterer and consequently, the priest, Joseph, must consider himself guilty for having blessed the adulterers and for having admitted them to the Eucharist." By "crowning adultery, the priest, Joseph, is in opposition to the teachings of Christ and has violated the law of God."[3] For Theodore, the Patriarch Tarasios had likewise to be condemned, since, although not approving of the new marriage, he had shown himself tolerant of it, avoiding both excommunicating the emperor and punishing the priest Joseph.

This behavior was typical of a sector in the Oriental Church, which proclaimed the indissolubility of marriage but in practice showed a certain submission to the imperial powers, thus sowing confusion among the peoples and stirring up protest from the most fervent Catholics.

Basing himself on the authority of St. Basil, Theodore claimed the faculty conceded to subjects of denouncing the errors of their superiors,[4] and the monks of Saccudium broke communion with the Patriarch because of his complicity in the Emperor's divorce. This triggered off the so-called "moicheian question" (from *moicheia,* adultery), which placed Theodore in conflict not only with the imperial government but with the Patriarchs of Constantinople themselves.

The following story is not very well known, but some years ago Professor Dante Gemmiti disclosed it through a careful, historical reconstruction based on the Greek and Latin sources,[5] which confirm that the ecclesiastical disci-

---

2. *Epist.* II, n. 181, PG 99:1559–60.
3. *Epist.* I, 32, PG 99:1015/1061C.
4. *Epist.* I, n. 5, PG, 99, coll. 923–24, 925–26D.
5. *Teodoro Studita e la questione moicheiana* (LER, Marigliano 1993).

pline of the Oriental Church in the first millennium still respected the principle of the indissolubility of marriage.

In September 796, Plato and Theodore, along with a certain number of monks, were arrested, imprisoned, and then exiled to Thessalonica, where they arrived on March 25, 797. In Constantinople, however, the population judged Constantine a sinner who continued to give public scandal, and due to the example of Theodore and Plato opposition increased day after day. Their exile was brief, as the young Constantine, following a palace conspiracy, had been blinded by his mother, who had taken upon herself the governing of the Empire. Irene called back the exiles, who moved to the urban Monastery of Studios along with most of the community of monks from Saccudium. Theodore and Plato were reconciled with the Patriarch Tarasios, who, after Irene's accession to power, had Constantine and *hegumen* Joseph publicly condemned for the imperial divorce.

Irene's reign was also brief. On October 31, 802, her minister, Nikephoros, proclaimed himself Emperor following a palace revolt. When Tarasios died shortly afterwards, the new *basileos* had a high-ranked imperial functionary elected Patriarch of Constantinople, who was also called Nikephoros (758–829). In a synod convoked and presided over by him, about the middle of the year 806, he reinstated *hegumen* Joseph (deposed by Tarasios) to his office. Theodore, who was then head of the monastic community in Studios— since Plato had retired to the life of a recluse—strongly protested the rehabilitation of *hegumen* Joseph, and when the latter took up his sacerdotal ministry again, he broke communion also with the new Patriarch.

The reaction was not late in coming. The Studios Monastery was occupied militarily; Plato, Theodore, and his brother Joseph (the Archbishop of Thessalonica) were arrested, condemned, and exiled. In 808, the Emperor convoked another synod, which met in January 809. It was this one that Theodore labeled *moechosynodus,* the "Synod of Adultery," in a letter of 809 to the monk Arsenius.[6] The Synod of Bishops recognized the legitimacy of Constantine's second marriage, confirmed the rehabilitation of *hegumen* Joseph, and anathematized Theodore, Plato, and his brother Joseph, who was deposed from his office as Archbishop of Thessalonica.

In order to justify the Emperor's divorce, the synod invoked the principle of the "economy of saints."[7] However, for Theodore there was no motivation that could justify the transgression of a divine law. Appealing to the teachings of St. Basil, St. Gregory of Nazianzus, and St. John Chrysostom, he declared the discipline of the "economy of saints," according to which a lesser evil could be tolerated in some circumstances, devoid of any scriptural basis.

Some years later the Emperor Nikephoros died in the war against the Bulgarians (July 25, 811) and another imperial functionary ascended to the throne: Michael I. The new *basileos* called Theodore back from exile, and he became the emperor's chief adviser. However, the peace was short-lived. In the summer of 813, the Bulgarians inflicted a very severe defeat on Michael I at Adrianople and the army proclaimed Leo V the Armenian (775–820) as Emperor.

When Leo deposed the Patriarch Nikephoros and had the veneration of icons condemned, Theodore led the resistance against iconoclasm. Indeed, Theodore is distinguished in the history of the Church not only as the opponent of the "Synod of Adultery" but also as one of the great defenders of sacred images during the second phase of iconoclasm. So on Palm Sunday of 815, it was possible to witness a procession of

---

6. *Epist.* I, n. 38, PG 99:1041–42.

7. A phrase in Byzantine theology referring to tolerance in praxis of that which is condemned in theory. To some extent it has parallels in Western concepts of "the lesser of two evils" and "gradualism."

a thousand monks of Studios, inside their monastery—but very much in view from the outside—carrying the sacred icons to the solemn acclamation of chants in their honor. The monks' procession triggered off a reaction from the police.

Between 815 and 821, Theodore was whipped, imprisoned, and exiled to various places in Asia Minor. Finally he was able to return to Constantinople, but not to his own monastery. He then settled with his monks on the other side of the Bosphorus, at Prinkipo, where he died on November 11, 826.

The "*non licet*" (Mt 14:3–11) with which St. John the Baptist confronted the tetrarch Herod for his adultery has resounded a number of times in the history of the Church. St. Theodore Studite, a simple religious who dared challenge the imperial power and the ecclesiastical hierarchy of his time, can be considered one of the heavenly protectors of those even today who, faced with the threats of changing Catholic practices on marriage, have the courage to repeat an inflexible *non licet*.

St. Bruno's
Filial Resistance
to Pope Paschal II[1]

A MONG THE MOST illustrious protagonists of Church reform in the eleventh and twelfth centuries, one that stands out is St. Bruno, Bishop of Segni and Abbot of Montecassino.

Bruno was born around 1045 in Solero, near Asti, in Piedmont. After his studies in Bologna, he was ordained a priest of the Roman clergy and enthusiastically adhered to the Gregorian reform. Pope Gregory VII (1073–1085) appointed him Bishop of Segni and numbered him among his most faithful collaborators. His successors Victor III (1086–1087) and Urban II (1088–1089) also availed themselves of the aid of Bishop of Segni, who combined his scholarly work with an intrepid apostolate in defense of the Primate of Rome.

Bruno participated in the councils of Piacenza and Clermont, at the time that Urban II proclaimed the First Crusade, and in the following years he was legate for the Holy See in France and Sicily. In 1107, under the new Pontiff, Paschal II (1099–1118), he became Abbot of Montecassino, an office that made him one of the most influential ecclesiastical figures of his time. A great theologian and exegete, resplendent in doctrine, as Cardinal Baronius writes in volume XI

---

1. Originally published in *Corrispondenza Romana* on March 4, 2015.

of his *Annals,* he is considered one of the greatest commentators on Holy Scripture of the Middle Ages.[2]

It was an age of political disputes and deep moral and spiritual crises. In his work *De Simoniacis,* Bruno offers us a dramatic picture of the disfigured Church of his times. Already at the time of Pope St. Leo IX (1049–1054):

> *Mundus totus in maligno positus erat* [the whole world was set in evil]: there was no longer any holiness; justice was failing and truth buried. Iniquity reigned, avarice ruled; Simon Magus possessed the Church, the bishops and priests were given over to sensual pleasure and fornication. The priests were not ashamed of taking wives, of celebrating their weddings openly and contracting nefarious marriages. . . . Such was the Church, such were the bishops and priests, such were some among the Roman Pontiffs.[3]

At the center of the crisis, besides the problem of simony and the concubinage of priests, there was the question of the investiture of bishops. The *Dictatus Papae* (1075), wherein St. Gregory VII had affirmed the rights of the Church against imperial demands, constituted the *magna carta* to which Victor III and Urban II referred in defending the rights of the papacy, but Paschal II abandoned the intransigent position of his predecessors and tried in every way to come to an agreement with the future Emperor Henry V.

At the beginning of February 1111, in Sutri, Italy, Paschal asked the German sovereign to renounce the right of investitures, offering him in exchange the Church's renunciation of all temporal rights and goods. The negotiations went up in smoke, and, yielding to the king's intimidations, Paschal

---

2. Réginald Grégoire, *Bruno de Segni, exégète médiéval et théologien monastique* (Italian Center for Studies on the High Middle Ages, Spoleto 1965).

3. *S. Leonis papae Vita,* in PL 165:110.

II accepted a humiliating compromise, signed at Ponte Mammolo on April 12, 1111. The pope conceded to Henry the privilege of the investitures of bishops with the ring and the crosier, which symbolized both temporal and spiritual power, prior to their pontifical consecration, and promised never to excommunicate the sovereign. Paschal then crowned Henry V as Emperor in St. Peter's.

This concession provoked a multitude of protests throughout Christendom, since it overturned the position of Gregory VII. According to the *Chronicon Cassinense*,[4] the Abbot of Montecassino protested vigorously against what he defined as not a *privilegium*, but rather a *pravilegium*, and promoted a movement of resistance against the papal compliancy. In a letter addressed to Peter, Bishop of Porto, he defined the treatise of Ponte Mammolo as "heresy," referring to the definitions made in many councils: "Whoever defends heresy," he writes, "is a heretic. Nobody can say that this is not heresy."[5] Elsewhere, speaking directly to the pope, Bruno states:

> My enemies say that I do not love thee and that I am speaking badly of thee behind thy back, but they are lying. I indeed, love thee, as I must love a Father and lord. To thee living, I do not desire another Pontiff, as I promised thee along with many others. Nevertheless, I obey Our Savior Who says to me: "Whoever loves father and mother more than me, is not worthy of me" (Mt 10:37). . . . I must love thee, but greater yet must I love Him who made thee and me.

With the same tone of filial candor, Bruno invited the pope to condemn the heresy, as "whoever defends heresy is a heretic."[6]

---

4. *Chronicon Cassinense*, in PL 173:868C–D.
5. Letter *Audivimus quod*, in PL 165:1139B.
6. Letter *Inimici mei*, in PL 163:463A–D.

Paschal II did not tolerate this voice of dissent and removed him from his office as Abbot of Montecassino. However, St. Bruno's example pushed some other prelates into asking with insistence for the pope's revocation of the *pravilegium*. Some years later, in a council that met at the Lateran in March 1116, Paschal II withdrew the agreement of Ponte Mammolo. The same Lateran Synod condemned the pauperistic conception of the Church expressed in the Sutri agreement. The Concordat of Worms (1122), entered into between Henry V and Pope Callixtus II (1119–1124), ended—at least momentarily—the fight over the investitures. Bruno died on July 18, 1123. His body was buried in the Cathedral of Segni, and through his intercession there were immediately many miracles. In 1181, or, more probably, in 1183, Pope Lucius III named him among the saints.

There are those who will object that Paschal II (like Pope John XXII later on with regard to the beatific vision) never fell into formal heresy. This, however, is not the heart of the problem. In the Middle Ages, the term "heresy" was used in a wide sense, while theological language would become more refined especially after the Council of Trent, with precise theological distinctions introduced among heretical propositions: near to heresy, erroneous, scandalous, and so on. We are not interested in defining the nature of the theological censures that would apply to Paschal II and John XXII's errors, but in establishing if it be licit to resist these errors. Such errors certainly were not pronounced *ex cathedra*, but theology and history teach us that if a declaration by the Supreme Pontiff contains censurable elements on the doctrinal level, it is licit and may be right and proper to criticize it, even if it is not a formal heresy, solemnly articulated. That is what St. Bruno of Segni did against Paschal II and the Dominicans in the fourteenth century against John XXII. They were not in error, but the popes of that time were, and in fact withdrew their positions before their deaths.

It should be stressed that those who most determinedly resisted the pope's deviation from the faith were precisely the most ardent defenders of papal supremacy. The opportunistic and servile prelates of that time adapted themselves to the fluctuations of men and events by placing the person of the pope before the Magisterium of the Church. Bruno of Segni, on the other hand, like many other champions of Catholic orthodoxy, placed the faith of Peter before the person of Peter and reproached Paschal II with the same respectful determination that Paul had directed to Peter (Gal 2:11–14). In his exegetical commentary on Matthew 16:18, Bruno explains that the foundation of the Church is not Peter, but the faith confessed by Peter. Christ, in fact, states that He will build His Church, not on the person of Peter, but on the faith that Peter manifested in saying: "Thou art the Christ, the Son of the living God." To this profession of faith, Jesus responds: "it is upon this rock and upon this faith that I will build My Church."[7]

By elevating Bruno of Segni to the honors of the altar, the Church endorsed his doctrine and his behavior.

---

7. *Comment. in Matth.*, Pars III, cap. XVI, in PL 165:213.

John XXII: A Pope
Who Fell into Heresy
and a Church That
Resisted Him[1]

AMONG THE MOST beautiful and mysterious truths of
our faith is the dogma of the beatific vision of the
souls in Heaven. The beatific vision consists in the
immediate and intuitive contemplation of God reserved for
souls who have passed to the afterlife in a state of grace and
have been completely purified of every imperfection. This
truth of faith, enunciated in Holy Scripture and confirmed
over the centuries by Tradition, is an irreformable dogma of
the Catholic Church. The new Catechism restates it in para-
graph 1023: "Those who die in God's grace and friendship
and are perfectly purified live forever with Christ. They are
like God forever for 'they see Him as He is' (1 Jn 3:2), 'face to
face' (1 Cor 13:12)."

At the beginning of the fourteenth century Pope John
XXII (r. 1316–1334) contested this thesis in his ordinary Magisterium and fell into heterodoxy. The most fervent Catholics
of that time corrected him publicly. "John XXII," Cardinal
Ildefonso Schuster wrote, "has the gravest responsibilities
before the tribunal of history [since] he offered the entire
Church the humiliating spectacle of the princes, clergy and

---

1. Originally published in *Corrispondenza Romana* on January 30,
2015.

universities steering the Pontiff onto the right path of Catholic theological tradition, and placed himself in the very difficult situation of having to contradict himself."[2] John XXII, whose baptismal name was Jacques Duèze, was elected to the papal throne in Lyons on August 7, 1316, after a *sede vacante* of two years following the death of Clement XV. He found himself faced with a turbulent period in Church history, between the "rock" of the French King Philip the Fair and the "hard place" of Emperor Louis IV the Bavarian, both adversaries of the primacy of Rome. So in order to reaffirm the supremacy of the Roman Pontiff against the audacious Gallicans and the tortuous secularists, the Augustinian Augustine Trionfo (1243–1328), by order of the pope, composed his *Summa de Ecclesiastica Potestate* between 1324 and 1328.

Yet John XXII entered into conflict with Church Tradition on a point of primary importance. In three sermons he gave in the Cathedral of Avignon between November 1, 1331 and January 5, 1332, he sustained the view that the souls of the just, even after their perfect purification in Purgatory, did not enjoy the beatific vision of God. Only after the resurrection of the flesh and the general judgment would they be raised by God to the vision of the Divinity. Placed "under the altar" (Rev 6:9), the souls of the saints would be consoled and protected by the Humanity of Christ, but the beatific vision would be deferred until the resurrection of their bodies and the general judgment.[3]

The error according to which the beatific vision of the

2. Alfredo Idelfonso Schuster, O.S.B., *Gesù Cristo nella Storia della Chiesa* (Benedictina Editrice, Rome 1996), 116–17. Cardinal Schuster was Archbishop of Milan during World War II and was beatified in 1996.

3. Marc Dykmans, in *Les sermons de Jean XXII sur la vision beatifique* (Gregorian University, Rome 1973), published the entire texts of the sermons of John XXII; cf. Christian Trottman, *La vision béatifique. Des disputes scolastiques à sa définition par Benoit XII* (Ecole Française de Rome, Rome 1995), 417–739.

divinity would be conceded to souls not after the first judgment but only after the resurrection of the flesh was an old one, but in the thirteenth century it had been rebutted by St. Thomas Aquinas, primarily in *De Veritate*[4] and in the *Summa Theologiae*.[5] When John XXII re-proposed this error, he was openly criticized by many theologians. Among those who intervened in the debate were Guillaume Durand de Saint-Pourçain, Bishop of Meaux (1270–1334), who accused the pope of re-proposing the Catharist heresies; the English Dominican Thomas Waleys (1318–1349), who as a result of his public resistance underwent trial and imprisonment; the Franciscan Nicholas of Lyra (1270–1349); and Cardinal Jacques Fournier (1280–1342), pontifical theologian and author of the treatise *De Statu Animarum Ante Generale Iudicium* [On the State of Souls Before the General Judgment].

When the pope tried to impose this erroneous doctrine on the Faculty of Theology in Paris, the King of France, Philip VI of Valois, prohibited its teaching, and, according to accounts by the Sorbonne's Chancellor Jean Gerson, even reached the point of threatening John XXII with burning at the stake if he did not make a retraction. John XXII's sermons *totus mundum christianum turbaverunt* [disturbed the entire Christian world], said Thomas of Strasburg, Master of the Hermits of Saint Augustine.[6]

On the eve of John XXII's death, he stated that he had expressed himself simply as a private theologian, without any intention of making a binding magisterial statement. Giovanni Villani reports in his *Chronicle* the retraction the pope made of his thesis on December 3, 1334, the day before his death, at the solicitation of Cardinal Bertrando del Poggetto, his nephew, and some other relatives.

4. *De Veritate*, q. 8, a. 1.
5. *Summa Theologiae*, I, q. 12, a. 1.
6. In Dykmans, *Les sermons*, 10.

John XXII: A Pope Who Fell into Heresy

On December 20, 1334, Cardinal Fournier was elected pope, taking the name of Benedict XII. The new Pontiff wanted to close the issue with a dogmatic definition and so issued the constitution *Benedictus Deus* on January 29, 1336, which included this statement: "We, with apostolic authority, define the following: According to the general disposition of God, the souls of all the saints ... already before they take up their bodies again and before the general judgment, have been, are and will be with Christ in heaven ... and these souls have seen and see the divine essence with an intuitive vision and even face to face, without the mediation of any creature."[7] This was referred to again as an article of faith on July 6, 1439, by the Bull *Laetentur Coeli* of the Council of Florence.[8]

In the wake of these doctrinal decisions, the thesis sustained by John XXII must be considered formally heretical, even if at the time he sustained it, the truth had not yet been defined as a dogma of faith. St. Robert Bellarmine, who dealt amply with this issue in *De Romano Pontifice*,[9] writes that John XXII supported a heretical thesis, with the intention of imposing it as the truth on the faithful, but died before he could have defined the dogma, and therefore without undermining the principle of papal infallibility by his behavior.

The heterodox teaching of John XXII was certainly an act of the ordinary Magisterium regarding the faith of the Church, but not infallible, as it was devoid of a defining nature. If we had to apply the Instruction *Donum Veritatis* (May 24, 1990) down to the letter, this authentic teaching, even if not infallible, should have been received as a teaching given by pastors, who through the Apostolic Succession speak "with the gift of truth" (*Dei Verbum* 8), "endowed by

7. Denzinger, n. 1000.
8. Ibid., n. 1305.
9. *Opera omnia* (Venetiis 1599), Book IV, chapter 14, columns 841–44.

the authority of Christ," "by the light of the Holy Spirit" (*Lumen Gentium* 25). His thesis would have required the degree of adhesion called "religious *obsequium* [submission, assent] of will and intellect, rooted in trusting divine assistance to the Magisterium," and thus "within the logic of faith under the impulse of obedience to the faith."[10] The defenders of Catholic orthodoxy, instead of resisting the pope's heretical doctrines openly, should have bowed to his "living Magisterium," and Benedict XII should not have opposed his predecessor's doctrine with the dogma of faith that declares that the souls of the just, after death, enjoy the Divine Essence with intuitive and direct vision.

But, thanks be to God, some good theologians and prelates of the time, moved by their *sensus fidei*, publicly refused their assent to the supreme authority. An important truth of our faith was thus able to be conserved, transmitted, and defined.

---

10. Msgr Fernando Ocáriz, *L'Osservatore Romano*, "On Adhesion to the Second Vatican Council," December 2, 2011.

When All of Europe
Was Excommunicated[1]

T HERE WAS A TIME when all of Christian Europe found
itself excommunicated, yet with no (known) heretic
in its midst. It all began on March 27, 1378, fourteen
months after Pope Gregory XI had returned to Rome from
Avignon to die. At the conclave, which took place in the Vatican for the first time in 75 years, sixteen cardinals participated, of the twenty-three then present in Christendom. Of
these, the great majority were French. This was a result of
the long period in Avignon.

On April 8, 1378, the Sacred College elected the Archbishop of Bari to the papal throne. Bartholomew Prignano, a
learned canonist of austere habits, was not a cardinal and so
was not present at the conclave. That same day, the people
burst into the conclave demanding the election of a Roman
pope, but the cardinals did not dare indicate that the election had already taken place and so pretended that the one
elected was old Cardinal Francesco Tibaldeschi, a native of
Rome. The following day, however, Bartholomew Prignano
was enthroned, taking the name Urban VI (1378–1389), and
on April 18, 1378 was duly crowned in St. Peter's.

It came to pass, though, that in the month of July twelve
French cardinals, along with the Aragonese Pedro de Luna,
met together in the city of Anagni, where on August 2 they
penned a *declaratio* wherein the Holy See was judged vacant
and the election of Urban VI invalid, as it had been extorted

1. Originally published in *Corrispondenza Romana* on July 13, 2016.

by the Roman populace through rebellion and tumult. On September 20, 1378, in the Cathedral of Fondi, Cardinal Robert of Geneva was elected as the new pope and took the name of Clement VII (1378–1394). After a vain attempt at occupying Rome, he was installed again in Avignon. Thus began the "Great Western Schism."

The difference between the Western Schism and the Oriental Schism, which from 1054 divided Christianity, is that the latter was a schism in the strict sense of the word, since the Orthodox refused and still refuse to recognize the primacy of the pope, Bishop of Rome and pastor of the Universal Church. The Western Schism, on the other hand, was a material rather than a formal schism, as there was no will on either part to negate the pontifical primacy. Urban VI and Clement VII, followed by their successors, were convinced of the legitimacy of their canonical election, and there were no doctrinal errors from either part in conflict. Today the Church assures us that the legitimate popes were Urban VI and those who followed him, but at the time it was not clear how to distinguish who the legitimate Vicar of Christ was.

From 1378, Christendom divided itself into two "obediences." France, Scotland, Castile, Portugal, Savoy, Aragon, and Navarre recognized Clement VII. Northern and Central Italy, the Holy Roman Empire, England and Ireland, Bohemia, Poland, and Hungary remained faithful to Urban VI. For more than forty years, European Catholics underwent drama on a daily basis. Not only were there two popes and two Colleges of Cardinals, but often in the same diocese there were two bishops, two abbots of each monastery, and two parish priests in each parish. Further, since the popes excommunicated each other, individual faithful Christians found themselves excommunicated by one pope or the other.

Even the saints were divided. Against St. Catherine of Siena and St. Catherine of Sweden (a spiritual daughter of St. Bridget), who supported Urban VI, were St. Vincent Ferrer,

Blessed Peter of Luxemburg, and St. Colette of Corbie, who adhered to the Avignon obedience. The situation was very confusing, and to say the least, it was difficult to find a way out of it.

On September 16, 1394, when Clement VII, the Avignon pope, suddenly died, the time to unravel the knot seemed to have arrived. All that was needed was for the French cardinals not to proceed with the election of a new Pontiff and for the pope of Rome, Boniface IX (1389–1404), the successor of Urban VI, to resign. Instead, the cardinals of Avignon elected a new pope, Pedro de Luna, an austere but obstinate man, who strongly asserted his rights and reigned for 29 years (1394–1423), under the name of Benedict XIII. Boniface IX's successors, on the other hand, were the "Roman" popes Innocent VII (1404–1406) and Gregory XII (1406–1415).

In the meantime, discussions continued to develop among theologians. The point of departure was the famous passage from the *Decretum Gratiani* that said: "Let no mortal man presume to accuse the pope of fault, for, it being incumbent upon him to judge all, he should be judged by no one, unless he is caught deviating from the faith" [*A nemine est judicandus, nisi deprehendatur a fide devius*].[2] The rule according to which nobody can judge the pope [*Prima sedes non judicabitur*] admitted, and admits, one sole exception: the sin of heresy. It was a maxim upon which all could agree and which could be applied to a heretical pope as well as a schismatic pope. But which one was guilty of schism?

In order to resolve the problem, many people fell into a gravely dangerous error: the doctrine of conciliarism, according to which a heretical or schismatic pope can be deposed by a council, as the assembly of bishops is superior to the pope. Leading exponents of this doctrine were the chancellor of the University of Paris, Pierre d'Ailly (1350–

2. Distinction 400, canon 6.

1420), and the Avignon cardinal and theologian Jean Gerson (1363–1429), also a chancellor and professor at the University of Paris.

This false ecclesiological thesis induced some cardinals of the two obediences to seek a solution in a general council that opened at Pisa on March 25, 1409, with the aim of inviting the two popes to abdicate, and to depose them if they refused, which is exactly what happened. The Council of Pisa declared itself ecumenical and representative of the entire universal Church and deposed the two rival popes as "schismatics and heretics," declaring the Roman See vacant. On June 26, 1409, the College of Cardinals elected a third pope, Peter Phillarges, Archbishop of Milan, who took the name of Alexander V; he was succeeded the following year by Baldassarre Cossa, who took the name of John XXIII. The true pope could only have been one of these three men, but at that time this was not clear to either the theologians or the lay faithful.

John XXIII, with the support of the German Emperor Sigismund (r. 1410–1437), took the initiative of calling a new council in the imperial city of Constance on November 5, 1414. His objective was that he be acknowledged as the one and only pope, with a confirmation of the Council of Pisa, from which he drew legitimacy. Towards this end he had created many Italian cardinals who supported him. In order to overcome the Italian majority, the French and the English succeeded in allowing the vote to be expressed not by *capita singulorum* [individuals], but by nations, that is, national groups. The right to vote was given to France, Germany, England, Italy, and (afterwards) to Spain: the five most important European nations. It was a profoundly revolutionary principle. In the first place, in fact, the nations—i.e., political entities rather than persons—entered too forcefully into the life of the Church, subverting the relationship of dependence they had always had with the Church. In the second place, and most of all, the principle according to which the pope is the supreme arbiter, moderator, and judge of the council was undermined, entrusting the deliberative decisions to the vote of the council fathers.

When John XXIII came to understand that the council did not want to confirm him as pope, he fled to Constance on the night of March 20, 1415, but was caught, deposed as a simoniac and public sinner, and excluded, like the other two claimants to the papal throne, from any future election. On April 5, 1415, the assembly published a decree known as *Haec Sancta* wherein it was solemnly affirmed that the council, assisted by the Holy Spirit, represented the entire Church Militant and had its power directly from God: therefore every Christian, including the pope, was obliged to obey it. *Haec Sancta* is one of the most revolutionary documents in the history of the Church, as it denies the primacy of the Roman Pontiff over a council. This text, first acknowledged as authentic and legitimate, was later reexamined by the papal Magisterium. It was completed, on a disciplinary level, by the decree *Frequens* of October 9, 1417, according to which ecumenical councils had to be rendered a stable ecclesiastical institution that would occur at regular intervals; as a consequence, councils represented "a kind of demand for control of the papacy," as the historian Hubert Jedin writes in his book *Ecumenical Councils of the Catholic Church*.

In this chaotic situation, the Roman pope, Gregory XII, consented to abdicate. This was the last renunciation of the pontifical throne before that of Benedict XVI. Gregory XII lost all pontifical prerogatives, as happens to a pope who, for extraordinary reasons, abandons the governance of the Church. The council recognized him as a cardinal and nominated him Bishop of Porto and stable legate to the district of Ancona, but Gregory died at the age of 90 at Recanati on October 18, 1417, before the new pope was even elected. The Avignonese pope Benedict XIII refused to renounce his claim to the papacy, but he was eventually abandoned by the countries under obedience to him and deposed as a perjurer, schismatic, and heretic on July 26, 1417.

The cardinals of the two obediences met together and on November 11, 1417 finally elected the new pope, Otto Colonna, a Roman, who took the name of Martin V in honor of the saint celebrated the day of his election; he would reign until 1431. The Great Western Schism was brought to a conclusion and peace appeared to have arrived in the Church, but the postconciliar period reserved bitter surprises for Martin V's successor.

Haec Sancta (1415):
A Conciliar Document
Condemned by the Church[1]

T HE COUNCIL OF CONSTANCE (1414–1418) is numbered
among the twenty-one ecumenical councils of the
Church, but one of its decrees, *Haec Sancta* of April
6, 1415, is considered heretical, as it asserts the supremacy of
the council over the Roman Pontiff.

At Constance, *Haec Sancta* was applied in the decree *Frequens* (October 9, 1417), which prescribed a council for five
years later, another after seven years, and then one every ten
years. With this, it attributed *de facto* to the council the function of a permanent collegial body that collaborated with the
pope and *de facto* was superior.

Martin V, elected pope at Constance in 1417, recognized in
the Bull *Inter Cunctas* of February 22, 1418, the ecumenicity
of the Council of Constance and all of its decisions, albeit
with the generically restrictive formula: "*in favorem fidei et
salutem animarum* [in favor of the faith and the salvation of
souls]." We do not know whether the pope had shared, at
least in part, the conciliarist theories or perhaps was obliged
to take this stance under pressure from the cardinals who
had elected him. *De facto* he did not repudiate *Haec Sancta*;
he applied the decree *Frequens* rigorously by fixing the date
of the new general council, which was held at Pavia-Siena
(1423–1424), and designated the city of Basel as the venue for

---

1. Originally published in *Corrispondenza Romana* on July 20, 2016.

the successive assembly. He died, however, on February 21, 1431, and the assembly opened under his successor Gabriele Condulmer, elected Pope Eugene IV on March 3, 1431.

At the very opening of the Council of Basel a dispute between two parties erupted: those loyal to the papacy and the partisans of the conciliarist theories, the latter making up the majority of the conciliar fathers. A tug-of-war resulted in various ups and downs. In the first phase, Eugene IV withdrew his approval from the rebel fathers of Basel. Subsequently, giving into political and ecclesiastical pressures, he backtracked with the bull *Dudum Sacrum* of December 15, 1433, revoking the dissolution of the council formerly decreed by him and ratifying the documents that it had published until that point and thus also *Haec Sancta*, which the Basel fathers proclaimed as their *magna carta*. But when he realized that they were still demanding more concessions, the pope repudiated the action of the council once again, transferring its location to Ferrara (1438), to Florence (1439), and afterwards to Rome (1443). The transfer was, however, rejected by the majority of the conciliar fathers, who stayed on at Basel, continuing their own council.

At this point the "minor" Schism of the West (1439–1449)—to be distinguished from the Great Schism (1378–1417) that had preceded it—commenced. The Council of Basel deposed Eugene IV as a heretic and elected Duke Amadeus VIII of Savoy as antipope with the name of Felix V. From Florence, where the council had been transferred, Eugene IV excommunicated the antipope and the schismatic fathers of Basel.

Once again, Christendom found itself split; but if the conciliarist theologians had prevailed at the time of the Great Schism, in this phase the pope was sustained by a great theologian: the Spanish Dominican Juan de Torquemada (1388–1468), not to be confused with the Inquisitor of the same name. Torquemada, decorated by Eugene IV with the title

Defensor Fidei, authored a *Summa De Ecclesia*, wherein he affirms with vigor the primacy of the pope and his *infallibilitas*.

In this work, he dissipates with great precision the ambiguities that had developed in the fourteenth century, starting with the hypothesis of a heretic pope. This case, according to the Spanish theologian, is concretely possible, but the solution to the problem should not be sought in any way in conciliarism, which negates pontifical supremacy. The possibility of heresy in a pope does not compromise the dogma of infallibility, as even if he wanted to define a heresy *ex cathedra*, his office would be lost at that very same moment.[2] Torquemada's theses were developed the following century by one of his Italian confreres, Cardinal Cajetan.

The Council of Florence was very important, as on July 6, 1439 it promulgated the decree *Laetentur Coeli*, which brought the Eastern Schism to an end, but also principally because it condemned conciliarism definitively by confirming the doctrine of the pope's supreme authority over the Church. On September 4, 1439, Eugene IV defined solemnly:

> We likewise define that the holy Apostolic See, and the Roman Pontiff, hold the primacy throughout the entire world; and that the Roman Pontiff himself is the successor of blessed Peter, the chief of the Apostles, and the true vicar of Christ, and that he is the head of the entire Church, and the father and teacher of all Christians; and that full power was given to him in blessed Peter by our Lord Jesus Christ, to feed, rule, and govern the universal Church, as is attested also in the acts of ecumenical councils and the holy canons.[3]

---

2. Pacifico Massi, *Magistero infallibile del Papa nella teologia di Giovanni de Torquemada* (Marietti, Turin 1957), 117–22.

3. Denzinger, n. 1307.

In the letter *Etsi Dubitemus*, of April 21, 1441, Eugene IV condemned the heretics of Basel and the "diabolical founders" of the doctrine of conciliarism: Marsilius of Padua, Jean of Jandun, and William of Ockham;[4] but towards *Haec Sancta* he took a hesitant stance, proposing what in modern terms might be defined as a "hermeneutic of continuity." In the decree of September 4, 1439, Eugene IV states that the superiority of councils over the pope, asserted by the Basel fathers on the basis of *Haec Sancta*, is "a bad interpretation given by the Basel fathers themselves, which *de facto* is revealed as contrary to the genuine sense of the Sacred Scriptures, of the Holy Fathers, and of the Council of Constance itself."[5] Eugene IV himself ratified the Council of Constance as a whole and in its decrees, exclusive of "any prejudice to the rights, dignity, and preeminence of the Apostolic See," as he wrote to his legate on July 22, 1446.

The "hermeneutic of continuity" thesis between *Haec Sancta* and the Tradition of the Church was soon abandoned. *Haec Sancta* is certainly an authentic act of a legitimate ecumenical council, ratified by three popes, but this is not enough to render binding on the doctrinal level a magisterial document posited against the perennial teaching of the Church. Today we view the matter thus: only those documents that do not damage the rights of the papacy and do not contradict the Tradition of the Church can be accepted from the Council of Constance. These documents do not include *Haec Sancta*, which is a formally heretical conciliar act.

Historians and theologians explain that *Haec Sancta* can be repudiated since it was not a dogmatic definition, inas-

---

4. *Epistolae pontificiae ad Concilium Florentinum spectantes* (Pontificio Istituto Orientale, Rome 1946), 24–35, especially at 28.

5. Decree of September 4, 1439, in *Conciliorum Oecumenicorum Decreta* (EDB, Bologna 2002), 533.

much as the typical formulas such as *anathema sit* are miss-
ing, as are terms like "order, define, establish, decree and
declare." The decree is really of a disciplinary and pastoral
nature and does not imply infallibility.[6]

The Schism of Basel ended in 1449 when Antipope Felix V
reached an agreement with Eugene IV's successor, Pope
Nicholas V (Tommaso Parentucelli, r. 1447–1455). Felix solemnly abdicated and the pope made him a cardinal and
papal vicar. The condemnation of conciliarism was repeated
by the Fifth Lateran Council, the Council of Trent, and the
First Vatican Council.

Those today who are defending the institution of the
papacy need to accompany the study of these dogmatic definitions with an in-depth analysis of the works of the great
theologians of the scholastic age in order to find all the elements necessary to tackle the present crisis in the Church.

6. See, for example, "Concile de Constance," Cardinal Alfred Baudril-
lart, in *Dictionnaire de théologie catholique*, 3:1200–24, especially 1221.

Adrian VI and Francis I
on the Throne of Peter[1]

THE CHURCH has a new pope, Jorge Mario Bergoglio: the first non-European pope, the first Latin American pope, the first pope called Francis. The mass media are trying to guess what will be the future of the Church during his pontificate by looking at his past as a cardinal, as Archbishop of Buenos Aires, and as a simple priest. What "revolution" will he bring about? Hans Küng has called him "the best possible choice."[2] But it is only after he has made his principal appointments and after his first programmatic speeches that it will be possible to predict the lines of Pope Francis's pontificate. What Cardinal Enea Silvio Piccolomini said in 1458 when he was elected with the name of Pius II is true for every pope: "Forget Enea, welcome Pius."

History never repeats itself exactly but the past helps us to understand the present. In the sixteenth century, the Catholic Church went through an unprecedented crisis. Humanism, with its immoral hedonism, had infected the Roman Curia and even the pontiffs themselves. Against this corruption there emerged Martin Luther's Protestant pseudo-reform, which was dismissed by Pope Leo X, a Medici, as "a quarrel between monks." The heresy had started to fizzle out when, on Leo X's death in 1522, the first German pope was elected: Adrian Florent from Utrecht, who took the name Adrian VI. The brevity of his reign prevented him from

1. Originally published in *Corrispondenza Romana* on March 14, 2013.
2. *La Repubblica*, March 14, 2013.

bringing his projects to fruition, in particular—as Ludwig von Pastor writes in *The History of the Popes*—"the gigantic war against the mass of abuses that deformed the Roman Curia and nearly the whole Church." Even if he had reigned longer, the evil in the Church was too entrenched, according to Pastor, "for one single pontificate to bring about the great change that was necessary. All the evil which had been committed over many generations could be corrected only by long and uninterrupted work."

Adrian VI understood the gravity of the evil and the responsibility for it of the men of the Church. This is clear from an instruction that his ambassador, Francesco Chieregati, read out in the pope's name at the Diet of Nuremberg on January 3, 1523. As Ludwig von Pastor says, this is a document of extraordinary importance not only for understanding the reformist ideas of Adrian VI, but also because it is a text unprecedented in the history of the Church.

After rebutting the Lutheran heresy, Adrian deals (in the last and most noteworthy part of the instruction) with the reformers' desertion of the supreme ecclesiastical authority.

Adrian VI gave Chieregati these express instructions:

You are also to say that we frankly acknowledge that God permits this persecution of His Church on account of the sins of men, and especially of prelates and clergy; of a surety the Lord's arm is not shortened that He cannot save us, but our sins separate us from Him, so that He does not hear. Holy Scripture declares aloud that the sins of the people are the outcome of the sins of the priesthood; therefore, as Chrysostom declares, when our Savior wished to cleanse the city of Jerusalem of its sickness, He went first to the Temple to punish the sins of the priests before those of others, like a good physician who heals a disease at it roots. We know well that for many years things deserving of abhorrence have gathered round the Holy See; sacred things have been misused, ordinances transgressed, so that in everything there has been change for the worse. Thus it is not surprising that the malady has crept down from the head to the members, from the popes to the hierarchy.

We all, prelates and clergy, have gone astray from the right way, and for long there is none that has done good; no, not one. To God, therefore, we must give all the glory and humble ourselves before Him; each one of us must consider how he has fallen and be more ready to judge himself than to be judged by God in the day of His wrath. Therefore, in our name, give promises that we shall use all diligence to reform before all things the Roman Curia, whence, perhaps, all these evils have had their origin; thus healing will begin at the source of sickness. We deem this to be all the more our duty, as the whole world is longing for such reform. The papal dignity was not the object of our ambition, and we would rather have closed our days in the solitude of private life; willingly would we have put aside the tiara; the fear of God alone, the validity of our election, and the dread of schism, decided us to assume the position of Chief Shepherd. We desire to wield our power not as seeking dominion or means for enriching our kindred, but in order to restore to Christ's bride, the Church, her former beauty, to give help to the oppressed, to uplift men of virtue and learning, and above all, to do all that beseems a good shepherd and a successor of the blessed Peter.

Yet let no man wonder if we do not remove all abuses at one blow; for the malady is deeply rooted and takes many forms. We must advance, therefore, step by step, first applying the proper remedies to the most difficult and dangerous evils, so as not by a hurried reform to throw all things into greater confusion than before. Aristotle says it well: "All sudden changes are dangerous to States."[3]

3. *Storia dei Papi*, vol. IV, 2, 87–88.

Adrian VI and Francis I on the Throne of Peter

Adrian VI's words help us to understand how the crisis in the Church today may find its origins in the doctrinal and moral failings of the men of the Church in the half-century that followed the Second Vatican Council. The Church is indefectible but her members, even the supreme ecclesiastical authorities, can make mistakes. They should be ready to recognize their faults, even publicly. We know that Adrian VI had the courage to undertake this revision of past errors. How will the new pope confront the process of doctrinal and moral self-destruction by the Church, and what will be his attitude towards the modern world, impregnated as it is by a profoundly anti-Christian spirit? Only the future will answer these questions, but it is certain that the causes of the obscurity of the present lie in our most recent past.

History also teaches us that Giulio de Medici succeeded Adrian VI and took the name of Clement VII (1523–1534). During his pontificate, on May 6, 1527, there occurred the terrible sack of Rome, perpetrated by Lutheran mercenaries (*Landsknechte*) of the Emperor Charles V. It is difficult to describe the devastation and sacrileges committed during this event, which proved to be more terrible than the sack of Rome in 410. Men and women of the Church were targeted for especial cruelty: nuns were raped, priests and monks were killed or sold as slaves, churches, palaces, and houses were destroyed. The massacres were swiftly followed by famine and plague. The population of Rome was decimated.

The Catholic people interpreted the event as a punishment they deserved for their own sins. It was only after the terrible sack that life in Rome changed profoundly. The climate of moral relativism dissolved and the general poverty stamped austerity and penitence onto the city. It was this new atmosphere which made possible that great religious rebirth, the Catholic Counter-Reformation of the sixteenth century.

The Sack of Rome (1527):
A Merciful Chastisement[1]

THE CHURCH is experiencing an era of doctrinal and moral disorientation. The schism has exploded in Germany, although the pope seems to be unaware of the significance of the drama. A group of cardinals and bishops advocate for agreement with the heretics. As always occurs in the darkest hours of history, events follow one after the other with extreme rapidity.

On May 5, 1527, an army descending from Lombardy reached the Janiculum. Holy Roman Emperor Charles V, enraged at Pope Clement VII's political alliance with his adversary, King Francis I of France, had moved an army against the capital of Christendom. That evening the sun set for the last time on the dazzling beauties of Renaissance Rome. About 20,000 men, Italians, Spaniards, and Germans —among whom were the Landsknecht mercenaries, of Lutheran faith—were preparing to launch an attack on the Eternal City. Their commander had given them license to sack the city. All night long the warning bell of Campidoglio rang out calling the Romans to arms, but it was already too late to improvise an effective defense. At dawn on the sixth of May, favored by a thick fog, the Landsknechts launched an assault on the walls, between St. Onofrio and Santo Spirito.

The Swiss Guards lined up around the Vatican Obelisk, resolute in their vow to remain faithful unto death. The last

1. Originally published in *Corrispondenza Romana* on December 3, 2015.

of them sacrificed their lives at the high altar in St. Peter's Basilica. Their resistance allowed the pope along with some cardinals the chance of escape. Across the Passetto di Borgo, the connecting road between the Vatican and Castel Sant'Angelo, Clement VII reached the fortress, the only bastion left against the enemy. From the height of the terraces, the pope witnessed the terrible slaughter that began with the massacre of those who were crowding around the gates of the Castle looking for refuge, while the sick of Santo Spirito Hospital in Sassia were massacred, pierced by spears and swords.

This unlimited license to steal and kill lasted eight days and the occupation of the city nine months. We read in a Venetian account of May 10, 1527, reported by Ludwig von Pastor: "Hell is nothing in comparison with the appearance Rome currently presents."[2] The religious were the main victims of the Landsknechts' fury. Cardinals' palaces were plundered, churches profaned, priests and monks killed or made slaves, nuns raped and sold at markets. Obscene parodies of religious ceremonies were seen; chalices for Mass were used to get drunk amid blasphemies; Sacred Hosts were roasted in a pan and fed to animals; the tombs of saints were violated; heads of the Apostles, such as St. Andrew, were used for playing football on the streets. A donkey was dressed up in ecclesiastical robes and led to the altar of a church. The priest who refused to give it Communion was hacked to pieces. The City was outraged in its religious symbols and in its most sacred memories.[3]

Clement VII, of the Medici family, had paid no attention to his predecessor Adrian VI's appeal for a radical reform of

2. Ludwig von Pastor, *The History of Popes*, vol. IV, 2 (Desclée, Rome 1942), 261.
3. See also André Chastel, *The Sack of Rome* (Einaudi, Turin 1983); Umberto Roberto, *Roma capta: The Sack of the City from the Gauls to the Landsknechts* (Laterza, Bari 2012).

the Church. Martin Luther had been spreading his heresies for ten years, but the Roman Papal States continued to be immersed in relativism and hedonism. Not all Romans, though, were corrupt and effeminate, as the historian Gregorovius seems to believe. Not corrupt were the nobles Giulio Vallati, Giambattista Savelli, and Pierpaolo Tebaldi, who hoisted a flag with the insignia *"Pro Fide et Patria"* and held the last heroic stance at Ponte Sisto. Nor were the students at Capranica College corrupt, who hastened to Santo Spirito and died defending the pope. It is to this mass slaughter that the Capranica College owes its title *"Almo* [Immortal]."

Clement VII survived and governed the Church until 1534, confronting the Anglican schism following the Lutheran one, but witnessing the sack of the city and being powerless to do anything was for him much harder than death itself.

On October 17, 1528, the imperial troops abandoned a city in ruins. A Spanish eyewitness gives us a terrifying picture of the city a month after the sack:

> In Rome, the capital of Christendom, not one bell is ringing, the churches are not open, Mass is not being said on either Sundays or feast days. The rich merchant shops are used as horse stables, the most splendid palaces are devastated, many houses burnt, in others the doors and windows broken up and taken away, the streets transformed into dungheaps. The stench of cadavers is horrible: men and beasts have the same burials; in churches I saw bodies gnawed at by dogs. I don't know how else to compare this, other than to the destruction of Jerusalem. Now I recognize the justice of God, who doesn't forget even if He arrives late. In Rome all sins were committed quite openly: sodomy, simony, idolatry, hypocrisy, and deceit; thus we cannot believe that this all happened by chance, but by divine justice.[4]

4. *Storia dei Papi*, vol. IV.2, 278.

The Sack of Rome (1527): A Merciful Chastisement

Pope Clement VII commissioned Michelangelo to paint the Last Judgment in the Sistine Chapel, conceivably to immortalize the dramas the Church had undergone during those years. Everyone understood that it was a chastisement from Heaven. There were no lack of premonitory warnings: lightning striking the Vatican and the appearance of a hermit, Brandano da Petroio, venerated by the crowds as "Christ's Madman," who on Holy Thursday, 1527, while Clement VII was blessing the crowds in St. Peter's, shouted: "sodomite bastard, for your sins Rome will be destroyed. Confess and convert, for in fourteen days the wrath of God will fall upon you and the city."[5]

The year before, at the end of August, the Christian army had been defeated by the Ottomans on the field of Mohács. The Hungarian King Louis II Jagiellon died in battle and Suleiman the Magnificent's army occupied Buda. The Islamic wave in Europe seemed unstoppable.

Yet the hour of chastisement was, as always, the hour of mercy. The men of the Church understood how foolishly they had followed the allurements of pleasures and power. After the terrible sack, life changed profoundly. The pleasure-seeking Rome of the Renaissance turned into the austere and penitent Rome of the Counter-Reformation.

Among those who suffered during the sack of Rome was Gian Matteo Giberti, the Bishop of Verona, though at that time he resided in Rome. Imprisoned by the besiegers, he swore that if he were freed, he would never again leave his episcopal residence. He kept his word and returned to Verona, where he dedicated himself fully to the reform of his diocese until his death in 1543. St. Charles Borromeo, who was afterwards the model for the bishops of the Catholic Counter-Reformation, would be inspired by his example.

5. Ibid., 247.

Gian Pietro Carafa and St. Cajetan of Thiene were also in Rome at the time of the sack. In 1524, they had founded the Theatine Order, a religious institute ridiculed for its intransigent doctrinal position and its abandonment to Divine Providence, even to the point of waiting for alms without ever asking for them. The two co-founders of the order were imprisoned and tortured by the Landsknechts and miraculously escaped death. When Carafa became a cardinal and president of the first Tribunal of the Sacra Rota and Universal Inquisition, he wanted another future saint alongside him, Father Michele Ghislieri, a Dominican. The two men, Carafa and Ghislieri, with the names Paul IV and Pius V, were to be the two popes par excellence of the Catholic Counter-Reformation in the sixteenth century.

The Council of Trent (1545–1563) and the victory of Lepanto against the Turks (1571) demonstrated that, even in the darkest hours of history, with the help of God, rebirth is possible: but at the origins of this rebirth was the purifying chastisement of the sack of Rome.

Paul IV (1476–1559) and the Heretics of His Time[1]

THE CONCLAVE that opened on November 30, 1549, after the death of Paul III, was certainly one of the most dramatic in the history of the Church. The English Cardinal Reginald Pole (1500–1558) was indicated by everyone as the great favorite. The pontifical robes were prepared for him and he had already shown someone his thanksgiving speech.

On December 5, Pole needed only one more vote to attain the pontifical tiara, when Cardinal Gian Pietro Carafa rose to his feet and in front of the astonished assembly accused him publicly of heresy, rebuking him, among other things, for having supported the crypto-Lutheran double justification theory, rejected by the Council of Trent in 1547. Carafa was known for his doctrinal integrity and pious life. The support for Pole collapsed, and after lengthy disputes, on February 7, 1550, Cardinal Giovanni del Monte was elected, taking the name of Julius III (1487–1555).

This accusation of heresy, the first to be launched in a conclave against a cardinal, reflected the divisions among Catholics in the face of Protestantism.[2] Between the 1530's and 1550's, heretical tendencies were being spread in the Roman ecclesiastical world and the party of "Spirituali" had

---

1. Originally published in *Corrispondenza Romana* on July 23, 2015.
2. See Paolo Simoncelli, *The Case of Reginald Pole: Heresy and Holiness in 16th-Century Polemics* (Editions of History and Literature, Rome 1977).

emerged, represented by ambiguous figures like Cardinals Reginald Pole, Gasparo Contarini (1483–1542), and Giovanni Morone (1509–1580). They cultivated an irenicist Christianity and intended to propose the reconciliation of Lutheranism with the institutional structure of the Roman Church.

Pole had created a heterodox circle of people well disposed to Lutheranism at Viterbo. Morone, while he was Bishop of Modena between 1543 and 1546, had chosen preachers who were subsequently all placed under process for heresy. The acts of the inquisitorial processes of Cardinal Morone (1557–1559), Pietro Carnesecchi (1557–1567), and Vittore Soranzo (1550–1558)—all of whom were part of the circle of "Spirituali"—published by the Italian Historical Institute for the Modern and Contemporary Age and the Vatican Secret Archives between 1981 and 2004 reveal just how thick this network of complicity was. It was vigorously opposed by two men, both destined to become popes: Gian Pietro Carafa, the future Paul IV, and Michele Ghislieri, the future Pius V. Both were convinced that the "Spirituali" were in reality crypto-Lutherans.

Gian Pietro Carafa, along with Gaetano di Thiene (St. Cajetan), had founded the Theatine Order and been chosen by Adrian VI to collaborate in the universal reform of the Church, interrupted by the premature death of the pontiff from Utrecht. We owe the institution of the Holy Office of the Roman Inquisition most of all to Cardinal Carafa. The Bull *Licet Ab Initio* of July 21, 1542, with which Paul III had instituted this organism, in accord with Carafa's suggestion, was a declaration of war on heresy. There were those who wanted to continue this war even to the extirpation of every error and those who wanted to end it for the sake of religious peace.

At the death of Julius III, in the conclave of 1555 the two parties clashed once again, and on May 23, 1555, Cardinal Gian Pietro Carafa was elected pope, overtaking Cardinal

Morone by a hairbreadth. He was seventy-nine years old at the time, and took the name of Paul IV. He was a pope without compromise who held the battle against heresies and true reform of the Church as his primary objectives. He fought against simony, imposed the residency of bishops in their own dioceses, reestablished monastic discipline, imparted a vigorous impetus to the Tribunal of the Inquisition, and instituted the Index of Forbidden Books. His right-hand man was a humble Dominican friar, Michele Ghislieri, whom he appointed Bishop of Nepi and Sutri (1556), cardinal (1557), and Grand Inquisitor for life (1558), thus opening for him the way to the papacy.

On June 1, 1557, Paul IV conveyed to the cardinals that he had ordered the incarceration of Cardinal Morone, under suspicion of heresy. He had charged the Inquisition to carry out the process and to bring the results of it before the Sacred College. Paul IV directed the same accusation against Cardinal Pole, who was in England and was removed from his office as legate. Cardinal Morone was imprisoned in Castel Sant'Angelo and freed only in August 1559, when, on the eve of his sentence, at the death of the pope, he regained his freedom and participated in the subsequent conclave.

In March 1559, a few months before his death, Paul IV published the bull *Cum Ex Apostolatus Officio*, in which he confronted the problem of possible heresy in a pope.[3] In it we read:

> Even the Roman Pontiff, who is the representative upon earth of God and Our Lord Jesus Christ, who holds the fullness of power over peoples and kingdoms, who may judge all and be judged by none in this world, may nonetheless be contradicted if he be found to have deviated from the Faith.

3. See *Bullarium diplomatum et privilegiorum sanctorum romanorum pontificum* (S. e H. Dalmezzo, Augustae Taurinorum, 1860), 6:551–56.

... If ever at any time it shall appear that any Bishop, even if he be acting as an Archbishop, Patriarch, or Primate; or any Cardinal of the aforesaid Roman Church, or, as has already been mentioned, any legate, or even the Roman Pontiff, prior to his promotion or his elevation as Cardinal or Roman Pontiff, has deviated from the Catholic Faith or fallen into some heresy: the promotion or elevation, even if it shall have been uncontested and by the unanimous assent of all the Cardinals, shall be null, void, and worthless.

This bull re-proposes the medieval canonical principle almost to the letter, according to which the pope cannot be contradicted nor judged by anyone, "*nisi deprehendatur a fide devius*"—unless he deviates from the faith.[4] There is debate on whether Paul IV's Bull is a dogmatic decision or a disciplinary act; whether it is still in vigor or if it has been implicitly abrogated by the Code of 1917; whether it applies to the pope who incurs heresy *ante* or *post electionem*, and so on. We shall not address these issues. The bull *Cum Ex Apostolatus Officio* is still an authoritative pontifical document confirming the possibility of a heretical pope, even if it gives no indication of the concrete procedure through which he might lose the pontificate.

After Paul IV, a cardinal who was more political than spiritual, Giovanni Angelo Medici di Marignano (1499–1565), was elected as Pius IV on December 25, 1559. On January 6, 1560, the new pontiff ordered the annulment of the process against Morone, reinstalling him in his former office and clashing seriously with Cardinal Ghislieri, whom he considered a fanatic of the Inquisition. The *Inquisitor maior et perpetuus* was deprived of the exceptional powers conferred on him by Paul IV and transferred to the secondary diocese of Mondovì. However, after the death of Pius IV, Michele Ghis-

4. Ivo of Chartres, *Decretales*, V, ch. 23, coll. 329–30.

lieri was unexpectedly elected on January 7, 1566, taking the name of Pius V. His pontificate was placed in complete continuity with Paul IV's, resuming inquisitorial activity again. Cardinal Morone, who as pontifical legate had been charged by Paul III to open the Council of Trent and at the mandate of Pius IV had directed the last sessions of the same, obtained the suspension of his sentence.

The history of the Church, even in times of her most bitter internal clashes, is much more complex than many think. The Council of Trent, which is a monument to the Catholic Faith, was inaugurated and then closed by a man gravely suspected of the Lutheran heresy. When he died in 1580, Giovanni Morone was buried in the church of Santa Maria Sopra Minerva in Rome (his tomb today is not to be found)—the same basilica in which St. Pius V, who initiated the process in support of the canonization for the champion of orthodoxy, Gian Pietro Carafa, Pope Paul IV, wanted to erect a mausoleum to Morone's accuser.

Not Only Heresy Offends
Against the Catholic Faith:
Auctorem Fidei (1794)[1]

I N A LONG INTERVIEW published in the German weekly *Die Zeit*,[2] Cardinal Gerhard Ludwig Müller, then Prefect for the Congregation of the Faith, raised a question of crucial relevance. When the interviewer asked the Prefect what he thought of those Catholics who attack the pope as "a heretic," he replied:

> Not only because of my office, but from personal conviction, I must disagree. A heretic in the theological definition is a Catholic who denies obstinately a revealed truth proposed by the Church that they are obliged to believe. It's another thing when those who are officially charged to teach the faith express themselves in a somewhat inappropriate, misleading, or vague way. The teachings of the pope and bishops are not above the Word of God, but serve it. . . . Moreover, papal pronouncements have different binding natures—ranging from a definitive decision pronounced *ex cathedra* to a homily used rather for spiritual analysis.

Today there is a tendency to fall into a simplistic dichotomy between heresy and orthodoxy. Cardinal Müller's words remind us that between black (open heresy) and white (complete orthodoxy) there is a grey area that theologians have explored with precision.

---

1. Originally published in *Corrispondenza Romana* on January 13, 2016.
2. *Die Zeit*, December 30, 2015.

Not Only Heresy Offends: *Auctorum Fidei* (1794)

There are doctrinal propositions, even if they are not explicitly heretical, that are condemned by the Church with theological qualifications proportional to their gravity and to their contrast to Catholic doctrine. Opposition to the truth in fact presents diverse levels, according to whether it is direct or indirect, immediate or remote, open or hidden, and so on. The "theological censures" (not to be confused with ecclesiastical censures or punishments) express, as Father Sisto Cartechini explains in his classic study, the negative judgment of the Church on an expression, an opinion, or an entire theological doctrine.[3] This judgment can be private, if given by one or more theologians independently, or public and official, if promulgated by the ecclesiastical authority.

Cardinal Pietro Parente and Monsignor Antonio Piolanti's *Dogmatic Theological Dictionary* sums up the doctrine thus:

The censure formulas are many, with a gradation that goes from the minimum to the maximum. Three categories can be identified. The first category regards the doctrinal content, as a proposition can be censured as (a) heretical, if it openly opposes a truth of faith defined as such by the Church; according to the greater or lesser opposition the proposition can be said to be near heresy, that it smacks of heresy; (b) erroneous in the faith, if it is opposed to a grave theological conclusion that derives from a revealed truth and a principle of reason; if it is opposed to a simple common sentence among theologians, the proposition is censured as temerarious. The second category regards the defective form for which the proposition is judged equivocal, dubious, insidious, suspect, evil-sounding, etc., even if not contradicting any truth of faith from a doctrinal point of view. The third category regards the effects a proposition can produce in particular circumstances of time or place, even if not erroneous in content and form. In such a

---

3. Sisto Cartechini, *Dall'opinione al domma. Valore delle note teologiche* ("La Civiltà Cattolica" Editions, Rome 1953).

case, the proposition is censured as perverse, corrupt, scandalous, dangerous, seductive for the simple.[4]

In all of these cases a presentation of Catholic truth lacks doctrinal integrity or is expressed in a deficient and improper manner.

This precision in qualifying errors was developed mainly between the seventeenth and eighteenth centuries, when the Church found herself faced with the first heresy that fought to remain internal: Jansenism. The Jansenist strategy, just like the modernists' later on, was that of continuing to self-proclaim their complete orthodoxy, despite repeated condemnations. In order to avoid an accusation of heresy, they engineered for themselves ambiguous and equivocal formulas of faith and morals, which did not frontally oppose the Catholic faith and allowed them to remain in the Church. With the same accuracy and determination, the orthodox theologians individually identified Jansenism's errors, branding them according to their specific characteristics.

Pope Clement XI (r. 1700–1721) in the bull *Unigenitus Dei Filius* of September 8, 1713 censured 101 propositions in the book *Réflexions morales* by the Jansenist theologian Pasquier Quesnel, as, among other things, false, captious, evil-sounding, offensive to pious ears, scandalous, pernicious, rash, injurious to the Church and her practice, insulting to the Church, suspected of heresy, and smacking of heresy itself, and, besides, favoring heretics, heresies and also schisms, erroneous and close to heresy.[5]

In his turn, Pius VI (Gianangelo Braschi, r. 1775–1799) in the bull *Auctorem Fidei* of August 28, 1794, condemned eighty-five propositions, extracts from the acts of the Jansenist Synod of Pistoia (1786). Some of these propositions

4. *Dizionario di teologia dommatica* (Studium, Rome, 1943), 45–46.
5. Denzinger, n. 2502.

from the synod are expressly qualified as heretical, but others are defined, according to the cases: schismatic, suspected of heresy, inducing heresy, favoring heretics, false, erroneous, pernicious, scandalous, temerarious, injurious to the common practice of the Church.[6] Each one of these terms has a different significance.

Thus the proposition in which the synod professes "to be persuaded that the bishop has received from Jesus Christ all the rights necessary for the good government of the Church" independently of the pope and councils (n. 6) is "erroneous and induces schism and subversion to the ecclesiastical hierarchal regime"; the one in which limbo is rejected (n. 26) is considered "false, temerarious, offensive to Catholic doctrine"; the proposition that prohibits placing relics or flowers on the altars (n. 32) is said to be "temerarious, injurious to the pious and recognized customs of the Church"; the one that hopes for a return to the archaic rudiments of the liturgy, "with the restoring of greater simplicity to the rites, expressing it in vulgar language, and uttering it loudly" (n. 33) is defined as "temerarious, offensive to pious ears, insulting to the Church, favoring the slander of heretics against the Church herself."

An analysis of the final *Relatio* of the 2015 Synod of Bishops, conducted according to the principles of Catholic theology and morals, can do nothing other than find grave discrepancies in that document with orthodox doctrine. Many of its propositions could be defined as evil-sounding, erroneous, temerarious, and so on, even if no one can say that it is formally heretical.

On January 6, 2016, a video message from Pope Francis diffused all over the world's social networks was dedicated to interreligious dialogue, where Catholics, Buddhists, Jews, and Muslims seem to be placed on the same level, as "chil-

6. Ibid., nn. 2600–700.

dren of [a] God" whom everyone encounters in their own religion, in the name of some common profession of faith and love. Francis's words, combined with those of the protagonists in the video and above all with the images, are the vehicle of a syncretistic message that contradicts, at least indirectly, the teaching regarding the redeeming uniqueness and universality of Jesus Christ and the Church, reaffirmed in the encyclical *Mortalium Animos* by Pius XI (1928) and the Declaration *Dominus Iesus* by the then-Prefect for the Congregation of the Faith, Joseph Ratzinger (August 6, 2000).

As ordinary baptized Catholics wishing to apply the theological censures of the Church to this video, we should have to define it as inducing heresy as far as the content is concerned, equivocal and insidious as far as the form is concerned, and scandalous as far as its effects on souls are concerned. The public and official judgment is up to the ecclesiastical authorities. No one is more qualified to speak out than the Prefect for the Congregation of the Faith.[7] Many distressed Catholics wish he would do just that.

7. At the time of original publication, the prefect was Cardinal Müller. He was removed from his post by Pope Francis in July 2017.

Can the Governing Acts of a Pope Be Questioned? Pio Bruno Lanteri (1759–1830)[1]

ANDRO MAGISTER has documented the wound inflicted on Christian matrimony by Pope Francis's two *motu proprios*[2] with an in-depth article,[3] which adds to Antonio Socci's comments in *Libero*,[4] Paolo Pasqualucci's on *Chiesa e Post Concilio*,[5] and my article in *Corrispondenza Romana*.[6] Confirmation that there is an atmosphere of deep unease in the Vatican has come from a dispatch of the news service *Die Zeit* of September 10, 2015,[7] concerning the dos-

---

1. Originally published in *Corrispondenza Romana* on September 18, 2015.

2. The Apostolic Letter *Mitis Iudex Dominus Iesus* and the Apostolic Letter *Mitis et Misericors Iesus,* both of September 8, 2015, pertain to the Latin Code of Canon Law and the Code of Canons of the Eastern Churches respectively.

3. See http://chiesa.espresso.repubblica.it/articolo/1351131bdc4.html?eng=y.

4. See https://rorate-caeli.blogspot.com/2015/09/socci-with-papally-mandated-catholic.html.

5. See http://chiesaepostconcilio.blogspot.com/2015/09/chi-ha-detto-che-nel-recente-motu.html.

6. See https://rorate-caeli.blogspot.com/2015/09/catholic-divorce-arrives-papal-marriage.html.

7. See https://www.zeit.de/gesellschaft/zeitgeschehen/2015-09/papst-vatikan-aufstand.

sier that is apparently circulating in the Vatican against the marriage annulment procedures of Pope Francis.

At this point a delicate problem is now placed before many consciences. Whatever judgment we have about the *motu proprios*, their content is nonetheless presented as an act of personal and direct government by the Supreme Pontiff. Can a pope be mistaken in the promulgation of ecclesiastical laws? Further, if someone dissents, is it not better to maintain an attitude of silence out of respect for the pope?

The answer comes to us from the doctrine and history of the Church. Many times, actually, it has happened that popes have been mistaken in their political, pastoral, and even magisterial acts without in any way undermining the dogma of the Roman Primate's infallibility. The resistance of the faithful to these erroneous and in some instances illegitimate acts by some supreme pontiffs has always been of benefit to the life of the Church.

Without going too far back into the past, I'd like to focus on an event of two centuries ago. The pontificate of Pius VII (Gregorio Chiaramonti, r. 1800–1823), like that of his predecessor Pius VI, went through periods of grievous tension and bitter struggles between the Holy See and Napoleon Bonaparte, the French Emperor. Pius VII signed a concordat with Napoleon on July 5, 1801, thinking that by doing so he was bringing an end to the era of the French Revolution; but Bonaparte proved very quickly that his real intention was to form a national church subordinate to himself. On December 2, 1804, Napoleon crowned himself Emperor (by his own hands) and a few years later invaded Rome again, annexing the Papal States to France. The pope was imprisoned and transferred to Grenoble and then to Savona (1809–1812).

The conflict increased with the Emperor's second marriage. Napoleon had married Joséphine Beauharnais on March 9, 1796. On the eve of the coronation, the Empress threw herself at the feet of Pius VII and confessed that her union with the Emperor had been only through a civil marriage. The pope then made it known to Napoleon that he would not proceed with the coronation until after a sacramental marriage. The marriage was hastily celebrated on the night of December 1 by Cardinal Fesch, Napoleon's uncle. Joséphine, however, did not give any heirs to Napoleon and her origins were too humble for the man who wanted to rule Europe by forming alliances with its sovereigns.

The Emperor then decided to have his marriage annulled in order to marry Maria Luisa of Austria, daughter of the most important European sovereign. In 1810, a *senatus consultus* dissolved the civil marriage and immediately after, the diocesan tribunal of Paris delivered a judgment of nullity on Napoleon and Joséphine's sacramental marriage. The Holy See did not recognize this declaration of nullity, made by obliging prelates, and on April 2, 1810, when the Emperor entered the Chapel of the Louvre for his second marriage to Maria Luisa, he found the places assigned to thirteen cardinals invited to the ceremony empty. The Emperor treated them as rebels and enemies of the state, since with this act they had wanted to express their conviction that his first marriage could be dissolved only by the pope. For this, the thirteen cardinals were condemned to abandon immediately their religious garments and insignia and dress as ordinary priests: from this comes the name "black cardinals" or "the zealous" (*zelanti*), in contrast with the "red" who were loyal to Napoleon and in favor of his marriage.

Pius VII wavered between the two tendencies, but on January 25, 1813, worn out by the fight, he signed a treatise between the Holy See and the Emperor where he accepted certain conditions incompatible with Catholic doctrine. The document, known as "the Concordat of Fontainebleau,"[8]

---

8. The text can be found in the *Enchiridion dei Concordati. Due secoli di relazioni tra Chiesa e Stato* (EDB, Bologna 2003), nn. 44–55.

accepted the principle of the Holy See's submission to the French national authority, effectively placing the Church in the hands of the Emperor.

This act, which was done publicly by the pope as Head of the Catholic Church, was immediately judged by contemporary Catholics as catastrophic and is still considered as such by Church historians. Father Ilario Rinieri (1853–1941), who dedicated three volumes to the study of the relations between Pius VII and Napoleon, writes that the Fontainebleau Concordat "was as ruinous for the sovereignty of the Roman Pontiff as it was for the Apostolic See,"[9] adding: "Why had the Holy Father Pius VII allowed himself to be induced to sign a treatise that contained conditions so ruinous? It was an occurrence in which the explanation goes beyond the laws of history."[10]

"The sense of foreboding and the dreadful effects that the publication of this Concordat produced are indescribable," recalled Cardinal Bartholomew Pacca (1756–1844) in his *Historical Memoirs*.[11] There was no scarcity of those who had accepted the Concordat enthusiastically, as well as those who, while criticizing it privately, did not dare express themselves publicly, out of servility or bad theological Catholic doctrine. Cardinal Pacca, Pro-Secretary of State to Pius VII, belonged instead to that group of cardinals who, after having tried in vain to dissuade the pope from signing the document, declared: "there was no other remedy for the scandal given to Catholicism and to the very grave evils that the implementation of that Concordat would have brought on

---

9. *Napoleon and Pius VII (1804–1813): Historical Reports on Unpublished Documents from the Vatican Archives*, vol. III (Unione Tipografico, Turin 1906), 323.

10. Ibid., 325.

11. *Memoriche storiche*, vol. I (Ghiringhello and Vaccarino, Rome 1836), 190.

the Church than an immediate retraction and general annulment of it entirely on the part of the pope," and in their letter
they included the well-known example from Church history
of Paschal II.[12]

The retraction arrived. Confronted with the protests from
the "zealous" cardinals, Pius VII, with great humility, realized his error and, on March 24, 1813, signed a letter to
Napoleon in which we find these words:

> Of that document, even if signed by Us, we will say to Your
> Majesty the same thing that was said to our Predecessor
> Paschal II in a similar case of a declaration signed by him
> containing a concession in favor of Henry V, of which his
> conscience had reason to repent, that is, "as We recognize
> that declaration as a bad deed, so We confess it as a bad
> deed, and with the help of the Lord, We desire that it be
> amended immediately so that no damage to the Church
> and no detriment to Our soul result from it."[13]

Knowledge of the retraction by the pope did not arrive
right away in Italy—only the matter of the signing of the
Concordat. Consequently, Venerable Pio Bruno Lanteri
(1759–1830), who led the movement *Amicizie Cattoliche*
(Catholic Friendships), immediately composed a letter
strongly criticizing the pope's act, and among other things,
he wrote: "I will be told that the Holy Father can do anything,
quodcumque solveris, quodcumque ligaveris, etc., this is true,
but he can do nothing against the divine constitution of the
Church; he is the Vicar of God, but he is not God, neither can
he destroy the work of God."[14] The Venerable Lanteri, who

---

12. *Memorie storiche*, vol. II, 88. See above, 35–39, "St. Bruno's Filial
Resistance."

13. *Enchiridion dei Concordati*, n. 45, 16–21.

14. *Scritti e documenti di archivio* (Edition Lanteri, Rome-Fermo 2002),
2:1019–37, especially at 1024.

was a strenuous defender of the rights of the papacy, admitted the possibility of resisting a pontiff in the case of error, knowing well that the power of the pope is supreme, but not unlimited and arbitrary.

The pope, like any other faithful Catholic, must respect the divine and natural law, of which he, by divine mandate, is the guardian. He cannot change the rule of faith nor the divine constitution of the Church (for example, the seven sacraments), just as any temporal sovereign cannot change the fundamental laws of the kingdom, since, as Bossuet recalls, in violating them "all the foundations of the earth are shaken" (Ps 81:5).[15]

No one could accuse Cardinal Pacca of excessively strong language or Pio-Bruno Lanteri of lacking attachment to the papacy. The concordats, like *motu proprio*s, apostolic constitutions, encyclicals, bulls, and briefs are all legislative acts that express the pontiff's will, but they are not infallible, unless the pontiff, in promulgating them, intends to define points of doctrine or morality in a binding manner for every Catholic.[16]

Pope Francis's pair of *motu proprio*s on the nullity of matrimony constitute an act of government that can be questioned and removed by a subsequent act of government. Benedict XVI's *motu proprio* on the traditional liturgy, *Summorum Pontificum* of July 7, 2007, was debated and strongly criticized.[17]

Pope Francis's pair of *motu proprio*s, his most revolutionary act of government yet, will not come into effect until

15. Jacques-Benigne Bossuet, *Politique tirée des propres paroles de l'Ecriture Sainte* (Droz, Geneva 1967 [1709]), 28.

16. Cf. R. Naz, *Lois ecclésiastique*, in *Dictionnaire de droit canonique* (Letouzey et Ané, Paris 1957), 4:635–77.

17. See, for example, the comparison of two voices, Andrea Grillo and Pietro De Marco, in *Ecclesia universa o introversa. Dibattito sul Motu proprio Summorum Pontificum* (Edition San Paolo, Cinisello Balsamo 2013).

Can the Governing Acts of a Pope Be Questioned?

December 8, 2015.[18] Is it illegitimate to ask that the synod question this matrimonial reform and a group of "zealous" cardinals (*zelanti*) request its abrogation?

18. This article was published on September 18, 2015; unfortunately, there is no evidence that any cardinal asked for its abrogation.

The 2014 Synod
and Vatican I[1]

THE HISTORICAL PHASE that has opened after the Synod of 2014 demands on the part of Catholics not only the willingness to debate and fight, but also an attitude of careful reflection and study toward the new problems up for discussion. The first of these problems is the relationship of the faithful with a Church authority that appears to be failing in its duty. Cardinal Burke in an interview with *Vida Nueva* on October 30, 2014 stated: "There is a strong sense that the Church is like a ship without a rudder." This is a powerful image, and it perfectly corresponds to the general picture.

The path to take in this confusing situation is certainly not that of taking the place of the pope and bishops in the governing of the Church, whose supreme helmsman in any case is Jesus Christ. Indeed the Church is not a democratic assembly, but a monarchical and hierarchical one, divinely established on the institution of the papacy, which symbolizes the irreplaceable stone. The progressivist dream of "republicanizing" the Church and transforming her into a permanent synodal state is destined to infringe upon the constitution *Pastor Aeternus* (December 8, 1870) of Vatican I, which defined not only the dogma of infallibility, but primarily the full and immediate power of the pope over all the bishops and the entire Church.

---

1. Originally published in *Corrispondenza Romana* on November 5, 2014.

In the discussions of Vatican I, the anti-infallibility minority, echoing the conciliarist and Gallican theses, affirmed that the authority of the pope did not reside in the pontiff alone, but in the pope as united to the bishops. A small group of council fathers asked Pius IX (r. 1846–1878) to affirm in the dogmatic text that the pontiff is infallible with the testimony of the Churches (*"nixus testimonio Ecclesiarum"*), but the pope revised the schema in the opposite sense, adding to the formula *"ideoque eiusmodi Romani Pontificis definitionis esse ex se irreformabilis"* the clause *"non autem ex consensu Ecclesiae"* [these definitions by the Roman Pontiff thus being irreformable in themselves, and not because of the consensus of the Church], to clarify definitively that the assent of the Church does not constitute the condition of infallibility. On July 18, 1870, before an immense multitude crowded in the Basilica, the final text of the apostolic constitution *Pastor Aeternus* was approved with 525 votes in favor and 2 against. Fifty-five members of the opposition abstained. Immediately after the vote, Pius IX solemnly promulgated the Apostolic Constitution *Pastor Aeternus* as a law of faith.

Pastor Aeternus establishes that the primacy of the pope consists in a true and supreme power of jurisdiction, independent of any other power, over all the pastors and over the entire flock of the faithful. He possesses this supreme power not by delegation on the part of the bishops or of the entire Church, but in virtue of divine right. The foundation of pontifical sovereignty does not consist in the charism of infallibility, but in the apostolic primacy that the pope possesses over the universal Church as successor of Peter and Prince of the Apostles. The pope is not infallible when he exercises his ruling power: the disciplinary laws of the Church, unlike those of divine or natural origin, can indeed change. Yet the monarchical constitution of the Church, which entrusts the fullness of authority to the Roman pontiff, is of divine faith, and thus guaranteed by the charism of infallibility. This jurisdiction includes, besides the power of government, that of the Magisterium.

The constitution *Pastor Aeternus* establishes with clarity the conditions of pontifical infallibility. These conditions were amply illustrated in the intervention of July 11, 1870 by Monsignor Vincenzo Gasser (1809–1879), Bishop of Bressanone and official speaker of the Deputation of the Faith. In the first place, Bishop Gasser specified that the pope is not infallible as a private person, but as a "public person." Furthermore, as a "public person" the pope must intend to fulfill his office, speaking *ex cathedra* as doctor and universal pastor; in the second place, the pontiff must express himself in matters of faith or morals, *res fidei vel morum*. Finally he must pronounce a definitive judgment on the objective matter of his intervention. The nature of the act that involves the infallibility of the pope must be expressed by the word *define*, which definition must be done using the term *ex cathedra*.

The infallibility of the pope does not mean in any way that he enjoys unlimited and arbitrary power in matters of government and teaching. The dogma of infallibility, while it defines a supreme privilege, is fixed in precise boundaries, allowing for infidelity, error, and betrayal. Otherwise in the prayers for the Supreme Pontiff there would be no need to pray "*non tradat eum in animam inimicorum eius* [that he may not be delivered into the hands of his enemies]." If it were impossible for the pope to cross to the enemy camp, it would not be necessary to pray for it not to happen. The betrayal of Peter is the example of possible infidelity that has loomed over all of the popes through the course of history, and will be so until the end of time. The pope, even if he is the supreme authority on earth, is suspended between the summit of heroic fidelity to his mandate and the abyss of apostasy that is always present.

These are the problems that the First Vatican Council

would have had to deal with if it had not been suspended on October 20, 1870, a month after the Italian army had entered Rome. These are the problems that Catholics bound to Tradition must study in great depth today. Without in any way denying the infallibility of the pope and his supreme authority in government, is it possible (and in what way) to resist him, if he fails in his mission, which is to guarantee the unaltered transmission of the deposit of the faith and morals consigned by Jesus Christ to the Church?

Unfortunately this was not the path followed by the Second Vatican Council, even if it proposed in some way to integrate and incorporate the teaching of Vatican I. The theses of the anti-infallibility minority, defeated by Pius IX, flourished once again in the halls of Vatican II, under the new form of the principle of collegiality. Thanks to some of the exponents of the *Nouvelle Théologie* like Father Yves Congar (1904–1995), after almost a century the minority of 1870 obtained a resounding victory. If Vatican I had conceived the pope as the apex of a *societas perfecta*, hierarchical and visible, Vatican II and especially various postconciliar actions redistributed power in the horizontal sense, imparting it to the episcopal conferences and synodal structures.

Today the power of the Church seems to have been transferred to "the people of God," which includes dioceses, parishes, movements, and associations of the faithful. Infallibility and supreme jurisdiction, subtracted from the pontifical authority, are being conferred upon the Catholic base, where Church pastors have to restrict themselves to the interpretation and expression of needs. The Synod of Bishops in October highlighted the catastrophic results of this new ecclesiology, which claims to base itself on a "general will" voiced through surveys and questionnaires of every kind. But what is the pope's will today, whose duty, through divine mandate, is the mission of guarding the natural and divine law?

What is certain is that in ages of crisis, such as the one we are experiencing, all of the baptized have the right to defend their faith, even by opposing non-compliant pastors. Authentically orthodox pastors and theologians, for their part, have the duty to study the extent and limits of this right to resistance.

The *Ralliement* of Leo XIII: A Pastoral Experiment That Moved Away from Doctrine[1]

Leo XIII (Gioacchino Pecci, who reigned 1878–1903) was certainly one of the most important popes in modern times, not only for the length of his pontificate (second only to that of Blessed Pius IX), but above all for the extent and richness of his Magisterium. His teaching includes encyclicals of fundamental importance, such as *Aeterni Patris* (1879) on the restoration of Thomist philosophy, *Arcanum* (1880) on the indissolubility of marriage, *Humanum Genus* (1884) against Freemasonry, *Immortale Dei* (1885) on the Christian constitution of states, and *Rerum Novarum* (1891) on the question of work and social life.

The Magisterium of Pope Gioacchino Pecci appears as an organic corpus, in harmony with the teachings of his predecessor Pius IX as well as his successor Pius X. The real turning point and novelty of the Leonine pontificate, by contrast, is in regard to his ecclesiastical politics and pastoral approach to modernity. Leo XIII's government was characterized, in fact, by the ambitious project of reaffirming the primacy of the Apostolic See through a redefinition of its relationship with the European states and the reconciliation of the Church with the modern world. The politics of *rallie-*

---

1. Originally published in *Corrispondenza Romana* on March 18, 2015.

ment, that is, of reconciliation with the secular and Masonic French Third Republic, formed its basis.

The Third Republic was conducting a violent campaign of de-Christianization, particularly in the scholastic field. For Leo XIII, the responsibility for this anticlericalism lay with the monarchists who were fighting the Republic in the name of their Catholic faith. In this way they were provoking the hate of the republicans against Catholicism. In order to disarm the republicans, it was necessary to convince them that the Church was not adverse to the Republic, but only to secularism. And to convince them, he argued that there was no other way than to support the republican institutions.

In reality, the Third Republic was not an abstract republic, but the centralized Jacobin daughter of the French Revolution. Its program of secularization in France was not an accessory element, but the reason itself for the existence of the republican regime. The republicans were what they were because they were anti-Catholic. They hated the Church as well as the monarchy, in the same way that the monarchists were anti-republican because they were Catholics who loved the Church as well as the monarchy.

The encyclical *Au milieu des solicitudes* of 1891, through which Leo XIII launched the *ralliement*, did not ask Catholics to become republicans, but the instructions from the Holy See to nuncios and bishops, coming from the pontiff himself, interpreted his encyclical in this sense. Unprecedented pressure was exercised on the faithful, even going as far as making them believe that whoever continued to support the monarchy publicly was committing a grave sin. Catholics were split into two currents, the "*ralliés*" and the "*réfractaires*," as had happened in 1791 at the time of the Civil Constitution of the Clergy. The *ralliés* accepted the pope's pastoral indications as they attached infallibility to his words in all fields, including those political and pastoral.

The *réfractaires*, with better theological and spiritual formation, on the other hand, resisted the politics of *ralliement*, maintaining that inasmuch as the papal intervention was a pastoral act, it could not be considered infallible and thus could be erroneous. Jean Madiran, who penned a lucid critique of *ralliement*,[2] noted that Leo XIII had asked the monarchists to abandon the monarchy in the name of religion in order to conduct a more efficacious battle in defense of the Faith—except that, far from fighting this battle, with the *ralliement* he effected a ruinous policy of détente with the enemies of the Church.

Despite the endeavor of Leo XIII and his Secretary of State Mariano Rampolla, this policy of dialogue was a sensational failure and unable to obtain its objectives. The anti-Christian behavior of the Third Republic increased in violence, culminating in the *Loi concernant la séparation des Églises et de l'État* on December 9, 1905, known as "the Combes law," which suppressed all financing and public recognition of the Church; it considered religion as belonging merely to the private sphere and not to the social; it mandated that ecclesiastical goods be confiscated by the state, while buildings of worship were given over gratuitously to *"associations culturelles"* elected by the faithful, without Church approval. The Concordat of 1801 that had for a century regulated the relations between France and the Holy See and that Leo XIII had desired to preserve at all costs fell wretchedly to pieces.

The republican battle against the Church, however, encountered a new pope along its way—Pius X, elected to the papal throne on August 4, 1903. With his encyclicals *Vehementer Nos* of February 11, 1906, *Gravissimo Officii Munere* of August 10 of the same year, and *Une Fois Encore* of January 6, 1907, Pius X, assisted by his Secretary of State Rafael Merry del Val (1865–1930), protested solemnly against the secular laws, urging Catholics to oppose them through

2. *Les deux démocraties* (NEL, Paris 1977).

all legal means, with the aim of conserving the traditions and values of Catholic France. Faced with this determination, the Third Republic did not dare activate the persecution fully, so as to avoid the creation of martyrs, and thus renounced the closing of the churches and the imprisonment of priests. Pius X's politics without concessions proved to be far-sighted. The law of separation was never applied with rigor, and the pope's appeal contributed to a great rebirth of Catholicism in France on the eve of the First World War. Pius X's ecclesiastical politics, the opposite of his predecessor's, represent, in the final analysis, a definitive historical condemnation of the *ralliement*.

Leo XIII never professed liberal errors; on the contrary, he explicitly condemned them. The historian, nevertheless, cannot ignore the contradiction between Pope Pecci's Magisterium and his political and pastoral stance. In the encyclicals *Diuturnum Illud, Immortale Dei,* and *Libertas,* he reiterated and developed the political doctrine of Gregory XVI and Pius IX; but the policy of *ralliement* contradicted his doctrinal premises. Leo XIII, far from his intentions, encouraged at the level of praxis those ideas and tendencies that he condemned on the doctrinal level. If we attribute the significance of a spiritual attitude to the word *liberal*, of a political tendency to concessions and compromise, we have to conclude that Leo XIII had a liberal spirit.

This liberal spirit was manifested principally as an attempt to resolve the problems posed by modernity through the arms of diplomatic negotiation and compromises, rather than with the intransigence of principles and a political and cultural battle. In this sense, as I have shown in my recent volume *The Ralliement of Leo XIII: The Failure of a Pastoral Project,*[3] the principal consequences of *ralliement* were of a

3. *Il ralliement di Leone XIII. Il fallimento di un progetto pastorale* (Le Lettere, Florence 2014).

psychological and cultural nature more than a political one. Those who sought to implement this strategy relied on the ecclesiastical "Third Party," which throughout the twentieth century tried to find an intermediate position between the modernists and the anti-modernists who were contending the issue.

The spirit of *ralliement* with the modern world has thus been around for more than a century now, and the great temptation to which the Church was exposed is still with us. In this regard, so great a teaching pope as Leo XIII made a grave error in pastoral strategy. The prophetic strength of St. Pius X is the opposite, in the intimate coherence of his pontificate between evangelical Truth and the life of the Church in the modern world, between theory and praxis, between doctrine and pastoral care, with no yielding to the lures of modernity.

Saint Pius X: On the Centenary of His Death[1]

O NE HUNDRED YEARS after his death, the figure of Saint Pius X (Giuseppe Sarto, r. 1903–1914) stands erect, majestic, and heavy-laden in the firmament of the Church. The sadness that clouds Pope Sarto's expression in his last photographs not only reveals a sense of the catastrophic consequences of the First World War, which had started three weeks before his death, but seems to foresee an even greater tragedy than the wars and revolutions of the twentieth century: the apostasy of nations and of churchmen themselves in the century that would follow.

The main enemy St. Pius X had to face had a name bestowed by the pontiff himself: Modernism. His relentless fight against Modernism characterized his pontificate indelibly and was a fundamental element of his sanctity. "The perspicuity and strength with which Pius X carried on the victorious struggle against the errors of Modernism," said Pius XII in his speech at the Canonization of Pope Sarto, "testify to what heroic degree the virtue of faith burned in his saintly heart."[2]

To the Modernism that proposed "a universal apostasy of the Faith and Church discipline," St. Pius X opposed an authentic reform that had its major point in the custody and transmission of Catholic truth. The encyclical *Pascendi* (1907), in which he struck down the errors of Modernism, is

1. Originally published in *Corrispondenza Romana* on August 27, 2014.
2. From the Address "Quest'ora di fulgente trionfo" of May 29, 1954.

the most important theological and philosophical document produced by the Catholic Church in the twentieth century. Yet St. Pius X did not limit himself to fighting the evil of the ideas, as if they were disincarnated from history. He wanted to strike at the historical carriers of these errors by imposing ecclesiastical censures, by watching over seminaries and pontifical universities, and by imposing the anti-modernist oath on all priests. This coherence between doctrine and pontifical praxis gave rise to violent attacks from "crypto-modernist" environments.

When Pius XII promoted Pope Sarto's beatification (1951) and canonization (1954), the latter was condemned by opponents influenced by the renewing ferments of their time as guilty of having repressed Modernism with brutal and police-like methods. Pius XII entrusted Monsignor Ferdinando Antonelli, a future cardinal, with the compilation of a historical *Disquisitio* dedicated to dismantling the accusations against his predecessor based on witnesses and documents. Today, however, these accusations appear once again even in the "celebration" by the writer Carlo Fantappiè that *L'Osservatore Romano* dedicated to St. Pius X on the centenary of his death, August 20, 2014.

Reviewing Gianpaolo Romanato's *Pius X: The Origins of Contemporary Catholicism*,[3] Professor Fantappiè, in his concern to disassociate himself from "the manipulations of the Lefebvrists," as he writes in an unfortunate way, using a term devoid of any theological significance, ends up identifying himself with the Modernist historians. He attributes to Pius X "an autocratic way of conceiving the government of the Church," along with

a basically defensive stance in regard to the establishment, with diffidence toward his own collaborators [some cardi-

---

3. Gianpaolo Romanato, *Pio X, le origini del cattolicesimo contemporaneo* (Lindau, Turin 2014).

nals, bishops, and clerics], whose loyalty and obedience he not infrequently doubted.... Availing himself of recent research in the Vatican archives, Romanato eliminates definitively those apologetic hypotheses that attempted to attribute responsibility for the police-like methods to close collaborators rather than directly to the pope himself.

These are the same criticisms that were aired some years ago in an article dedicated to Pius X, "The Scourge of Modernists," by Alberto Melloni, according to whom "the archives permit us to document the spirit in which Pius X was a conscious and active part of the institutional violence carried out by the anti-modernists."[4]

The basic problem, according to Fantappiè, would not then be "the method by which modernism was repressed, but rather the timeliness and validity of the condemnation." St. Pius's vision "had been surpassed" by history, since he did not understand the developments of theology and ecclesiology in the twentieth century. His papacy is seen as basically having a dialectic role of an antithesis with respect to the theses of "theological modernity." Fantappiè concludes that Pius X's role was that of "ferrying Catholicism from the structures and mentality of the Restoration to juridical and pastoral institutional modernity."

In an attempt to sort out this confusion, we may turn to a volume by Cristina Siccardi, *St. Pius X: The Life of the Pope Who Ordered and Reformed the Church*,[5] which includes a valuable foreword by His Eminence Cardinal Raymond Burke, former Prefect of the Supreme Tribunal of the Apostolic Signatura. The cardinal recalls that from his very first encyclical letter of October 4, 1903, *E Supremi Apostolatus*, St. Pius X indicated the program of his pontificate, which faced

---

4. *Corriere della Sera*, August 23, 2006.
5. Cristina Siccardi, *San Pio X. Vita del Papa che ha ordinato e riformato la Chiesa* (Edizioni San Paolo, Roma 2014).

a state of confusion in the world, errors about the Faith in the Church, and loss of the faith on the part of many. He opposed this apostasy with the words of St. Paul: "*Instaurare omnia in Christo*," to restore all things in Christ. "*Instaurare omnia in Christo*," Cardinal Burke writes, "is the sum total of St. Pius X's pontificate: everything was aimed at the re-Christianizing of society assailed by liberal relativism, which trampled on the rights of God in the name of a 'science' freed from any type of relationship with the Creator."[6]

St. Pius X's was most of all a work of catechesis, since he understood that widespread errors needed to be countered by imparting knowledge of the Faith at a deeper level than ever to the most simple, starting with children. Toward the end of 1912, his desire became reality with the publication of the Catechism that bears his name, destined originally for the diocese of Rome, but afterwards diffused in every diocese of Italy and the world at large.

The colossal reforming and restoring work of St. Pius X was carried out under the incomprehension of the ecclesiastical world itself. "St. Pius X," writes Cristina Siccardi, "did not look for the approval of the Roman Curia, the priests, the bishops, the cardinals, or the faithful, and most of all he did not look for the approval of the world, but always and only did he look for the approval of God, at the risk of damaging his public image, and doing thus, he undoubtedly made many enemies while alive, and even more in death."[7]

Today we may say that his worst enemies are not those who attack him openly, but those who try to diminish the importance of his work, making him a precursor of the conciliar and postconciliar reforms.

The daily newspaper *La Tribuna di Treviso* informs us that on the occasion of the centenary of St. Pius X's death, "the

---

6. Cardinal Burke, Foreword to *San Pio X*, 9.
7. *San Pio X*, 25.

Diocese of Treviso opened its doors to divorced and cohabiting couples," inviting them, in five churches—among them the church of Riese, birthplace of Pope Giuseppe Sarto—to pray for a good outcome at the October Synod on the Family, for which Cardinal Kasper laid down the lines in his report at the Consistory of February 20, 2014.

To make St. Pius X the precursor of Cardinal Kasper is an affront that transforms Melloni's contemptuous label "the scourge of Modernists" into a compliment.

The Worldwide Impact and Significance of the *Correctio filialis*[1]

T HE "FILIAL CORRECTION" addressed to Pope Francis by more than 60 priests and scholars of the Church has had an extraordinary impact all over the world.[2] There was no lack of those who tried to minimize the significance of the initiative, declaring the number of signatories to be limited and marginal. Yet if the initiative is irrelevant, why has it been so widely reported in all the media outlets of the five continents, including countries like Russia and China? Steve Skojec of *OnePeterFive* reported that a search on Google News resulted in more than 5,000 news articles, while there were 100,000 visits to the site www.correctiofilialis.org in a space of 48 hours.

It is essential to acknowledge that the reason for this worldwide echo is one only: the truth can be ignored or repressed, but when it is made manifest with clarity it has its own intrinsic power and is destined to spread by itself. The main enemy of truth is not error, but ambiguity. The cause of the diffusion of errors and heresies in the Church is not due to the strength of these errors, but the culpable silence of those who should openly defend the truth of the Gospel.

---

1. Originally published in *Corrispondenza Romana* on September 27, 2017.
2. In the end, the *Correctio filialis* gained the signatures of 250 scholars and pastors around the world. The document and the list of signatories may be found at www.correctiofilialis.org.

The truth asserted by the "filial correction" is that Pope Francis, through a long series of words, acts, and omissions, "has upheld, directly or indirectly, and, with what degree of awareness we do not seek to judge, both by public office and by private act propagated in the Church [seven] false and heretical propositions." The signatories insist respectfully that the pope "publicly reject these propositions, thus accomplishing the mandate of our Lord Jesus Christ given to St. Peter and through him to all his successors until the end of the world: 'I have prayed for thee, that thy faith fail not: and thou, being once converted, confirm thy brethren.'"

No reply regarding the correction has yet arrived; only clumsy attempts at disqualifying or singling out the signatories, with particular aim at some of the most well known, like the former President of the Vatican Bank, Ettore Gotti Tedeschi. In reality, as Gotti Tedeschi himself said in an interview with Marco Tosatti on September 24, 2017, the authors of the *Correctio* have acted out of love for the Church and the papacy. Gotti Tedeschi and another well-known signatory, German writer Martin Mosebach, were both applauded last September 14 at the Angelicum by a group of over 400 priests and laypeople including three cardinals and several bishops, on the occasion of the convention celebrating the tenth anniversary of the *motu proprio Summorum Pontificum*.

Two other signatories, Professors Claudio Pierantoni and Anna Silva, expressed the same ideas found in the *Correctio* at a meeting on the theme *"Let's Clarify,"* organized on April 23, 2017, by the Italian Catholic news agency *La Nuova Bussola Quotidiana*, supported by other prelates, among whom was the late Cardinal Carlo Caffara. Many other signatories of the document occupy or have occupied prominent positions in ecclesiastical institutions. Others again are distinguished university professors. If the authors of the *Correctio* were isolated in the Catholic world, their document would not have had the resonance it attained.

Worldwide Impact of the *Correctio filialis*

A *Filial Appeal* to Pope Francis in 2015 was signed by around 900,000 people from all over the world, and a *Declaration of Fidelity to the Unchangeable Teaching of the Church on Matrimony*, presented in 2015 by 80 Catholic luminaries, gathered 35,000 signatures. In 2016 four cardinals formulated their *dubia* about the Apostolic Exhortation *Amoris Laetitia*. In the meantime, scandals of an economic and moral nature are undermining Pope Francis's pontificate. The American Vaticanist John Allen, certainly not of a traditional bent, revealed in *Crux* on September 25, 2017 how difficult his position has become.

Among the most ridiculous accusations that are being made against the signatories of the document is that they are "Lefebvrists," since among them is Bishop Bernard Fellay, the Superior of the Fraternity of St. Pius X. Monsignor Fellay's adhesion to a document of this type is a historical act, which clarifies without the shadow of a doubt the Fraternity's position in regard to the new pontificate. However, "Lefebvrism" is a verbal locution that has for the progressives the same role the word "fascism" had for the Communists in the 1970's: discredit the adversary without discussing the reasons. The presence of Bishop Fellay is, moreover, reassuring for all the signatories of the *Correctio*. How can the pope not have the same comprehension and benevolence towards them that he has shown over the last two years towards the Fraternity of St. Pius X?

The Archbishop of Chieti, Bruno Forte, previously special secretary to the Bishops' Synod on the Family, declared that the *Correctio* represents "a prejudicially closed stance towards the spirit of the Second Vatican Council that Pope Francis is incarnating so profoundly."[3] In the same Italian bishops' newspaper, Monsignor Lorizio writes that the spirit of Vatican II, incarnated in Pope Francis, consists in the primacy of

3. *Avvenire*, September 26, 2015.

99

the pastoral over the theological; in other words, in the subordination of the natural law to life experience, since, as he explains, "the pastoral comprises and includes theology" and not vice versa. Monsignor Lorizio teaches theology at the same Faculty of the Lateran University whose Dean used to be Monsignor Brunero Gherardini (1925–2017), who died on September 22, 2017, on the eve of the *Correctio* he was unable to sign because of his precarious health condition.

This great exponent of the Roman Theological School demonstrated in his most recent books what a deplorable landing place we have been brought to by the primacy of the pastoral announced at Vatican II and propagated by its ultra-progressive interpreters, among whom Forte, the makeshift theologian Massimo Faggioli, and also Alberto Melloni are all distinguishing themselves with their flimsy attacks on the *Correctio.*

Bishop Forte added that the document is an operation that cannot be supported by "those who are faithful to the successor of Peter whom they recognize as the pastor the Lord has given to the Church as the guide of universal communion. Fidelity should always be directed to the living God, who speaks to the Church today through the pope." So now we have come to the point of defining Pope Francis a "living God," forgetting that the Church is founded on Jesus Christ, whom the pope represents on earth; the pope is not the divine Master of the Church. As Antonio Socci correctly wrote, the pope is not a "second Jesus"[4] but the 266th successor to Peter. His mandate is not that of changing or "improving" the words of Our Lord but of guarding and transmitting them in the most faithful manner. If this doesn't happen, Catholics have the duty to reprove him in a filial way, following the example of St. Paul in regard to the Prince of the Apostles, Peter (Gal 2:11).

4. *Libero*, September 24, 2017.

Lastly, there are those surprised that Cardinals Walter Brandmüller and Raymond Leo Burke did not sign the document, ignoring, as *Rorate Caeli* underlined, that the *Correctio* of the Sixty is of a purely theological nature, whereas the one of the cardinals, when it comes, will have much more authority and importance, also on the canonical level. Fraternal correction, foreseen by the Gospel and current Canon Law (in canon 212, par. 3), can have different forms. In an interview with Maike Hickson, Bishop Athanasius Schneider declared:

> This principle of fraternal correction inside the Church has been valid for all time, even with regard to the pope, and so it should be valid also in our times. Unfortunately, these days anyone who dares speak the truth—even if he does so respectfully with regard to the Shepherds of the Church—is classified as an enemy of unity, as happened to St. Paul, when he declared: "Am I then become your enemy, because I tell you the truth?" (Gal 4:16).

PART II

LECTURES

Resistance and Fidelity to the Church in Times of Crisis[1]

The infallibility and indefectibility of the Church

THE CHURCH has been through the gravest crises in the course of her history: external persecutions like those that characterized the first three centuries of her life and since then have always accompanied her, as well as internal crises such as Arianism in the fourth century and the Great Western Schism. However, the process of the Church's "auto-demolition," "struck by those who belong to her," which Paul VI spoke of as far back as 1968,[2] appears to be a crisis without precedent because of its extent and depth.

We say this in a spirit of deep love for the papacy, rejecting every form of anti-infallibility, Gallicanism, and conciliarism—in a word, every error that would diminish the role and mission of the papacy. We profess with the entire Church that there is no higher authority on earth than that of the pope, since there is no mission or office more elevated than his. Jesus Christ, in the person of Peter and his successors, conferred upon the Roman Pontiff the mission to be the visible head of the Church and his vicar.[3] The dogmatic constitution *Pastor Aeternus* of the First Vatican Council

1. A lecture given in Florence, Italy, on October 2, 2016.
2. Paul VI, *Discourse to Lombard Seminary in Rome*, December 7, 1968, in *Insegnamenti*, vol. VI (1968), 1188–89.
3. See my synthesis *Il Vicario di Cristo. Il Papato tra normalità ed eccezione* (Fede e Cultura, Verona 2012).

defined the dogmas of the Roman primacy and papal infalli-bility.[4] The first asserts that the pope has supreme power of jurisdiction, both ordinary and immediate, over individual Churches, individual pastors, and all the faithful. The second dogma teaches that the pope is infallible when he speaks *ex cathedra*, which is to say when in his function as supreme pastor he defines that a doctrine in matters of faith or mor-als must be held by the entire Church.

The authority of the pope has precise limits, however, which cannot be ignored. Javier Hervada in his well-known manual on constitutional canon law writes: "The power of the pope is not unlimited: it is circumscribed within deter-mined limits. The limits may regard the validity or the law-fulness of his exercise of power. The limits regarding validity are given as: a) of the natural law; b) of the positive divine law; c) of the nature and the ends of the Church."[5]

If the pope oversteps these limits he deviates from the Catholic Faith. It is common doctrine that the pope as a pri-vate doctor may deviate from the Catholic Faith, falling into heresy.[6] The hypothesis of a heretic pope is treated as a *scho-lion* in all theological treatises.[7]

It should be emphasized that the expression "private doc-tor" does not refer to the Supreme Pontiff's acts of a private nature, but to his "public" function as "supreme pastor of the Church."[8] In his final *relatio* on the dogma of infallibility

---

4. Vatican Council I, Sess. IV, quoted in Denzinger, nn. 3059–75.

5. Javier Hervada, *Diritto costituzionale canonico* (Giuffré, Rome 1989), 273.

6. See the recent studies of Arnaldo Xavier Vidigal da Silveira, *Ipotesi teologica di un Papa eretico* (Solfanelli, Chieti 2016); Robert Siscoe and John Salza, *True or False Pope? Refuting Sedevacantism and Other Modern Errors* (STAS Editions, Winona, MN 2015).

7. See, for example, Charles Journet, *L'Eglise du Verbe incarné* (Desclée de Brouwer, Paris 1941), 1:626 and 2:839–41.

8. Umberto Betti, *The Dogmatic Constitution* Pastor Aeternus *of the First Vatican Council* (Pontificio Ateneo Antoniano, Rome 1961), 644–46.

at the First Vatican Council, Monsignor Vincenzo Gasser (1809–1879), representative of the Deputation of the Faith [the doctrinal commission of that council], stated precisely that the pope is considered a "public person" only if he is speaking *ex cathedra*, with the intention of binding the Church to his teaching.[9] The theological hypothesis of a heretical pope does not contradict the dogma of infallibility, since the infallibility concerns the person of the pope only when he acts *ex cathedra*. Further, those who deny that the pope can fall into heresy still admit the possibility that he can express himself in an erroneous, misleading, or scandalous manner. If the problem of a heretic pope poses the problem of the loss of the pontificate, the presence of a pope *fautor haeresim*[10] poses equally grave theological problems.

In order to better clarify this question, we must remember that alongside the dogma of the Roman primacy and papal infallibility a third exists, not yet defined by the solemn Magisterium, but in a certain sense the origin of the previous two: the dogma of the indefectibility of the Church.

Indefectibility is the supernatural property of the Church, and thanks to this she will never disappear, but will arrive at the end of time identical to herself, with no change in her permanent essence, that is, her dogmas, rites (the Mass and

---

9. "*Pontifex dicitur infallibilis cum loquitur ex cathedra ... scilicet quando ... primo non tanquam doctor privatus ... aliquid decernit, sed docet supremi omnium christianorum pastori set doctoris munere fungens*" (Mansi, 52:1225C). The words we will find again in the dogmatic definition: "*cum ex cathedra loquitur, id est cum omnium christianorum pastoris et doctoris munere fungens.*"

10. Meaning a promoter of heresy, although not formally a heretic. On the notes of doctrinal censure below the level of heresy, see Antonio Piolanti and Pietro Parente, *Dizionario di teologia dommatica*; Lucien Choupin, *Valeurs des décisions doctrinales et disciplinaires du Saint-Siège* (Beauchesne, Paris 1913); H. Quilliet, *Censures doctrinales*, in *Dictionnaire de théologie catholique*, 2:2101–13; Marino Mosconi, *Magistero autentico non infallibile e protezione penale* (Edizioni Glossa, Milan-Rome 1996).

the sacraments), and the apostolic succession of her hierarchy. The Augustinian theologian Martin Jugie (1858–1954), in the *Catholic Encyclopedia* entry dedicated to indefectibility, writes that this is a truth of the faith clearly contained in Holy Scripture and taught by the ordinary Magisterium.[11] Modernism opposed the indefectibility of the Church, and had (and still has) theological and philosophical evolutionism as its basis.[12]

Indefectibility includes not only the infallibility of the pope, but that of the entire Church. The pope is, under certain conditions, infallible but not indefectible. The Church, which includes the pope, bishops, and ordinary laypeople, is infallible and indefectible. Theology differentiates between essential or absolute infallibility and shared or relative infallibility: the first belongs to God "*qui nec falli nec fallere potest* [who can neither deceive nor be deceived];"[13] the second is the charism bestowed by God on His Church.

From the First Vatican Council onwards the infallibility of the pope has been greatly discussed, whether by way of affirmation or of denial. Little to nothing has been said about the indefectibility and the infallibility of the Church. Yet the combination of papal infallibility and the infallibility of the Church, notes Monsignor Brunero Gherardini, is conformable to Tradition and was confirmed by Vatican I:

> [F]aithfully adhering to the tradition received from the beginning of the Christian faith, to the glory of God our

---

11. Martin Jugie et al., "Indefettibilità," in *Enciclopedia cattolica*, vol. VI (Città del Vaticano 1951), 1792–94. Father Jugie records that the First Vatican Council had prepared a definition schema regarding this question.

12. The decree *Lamentabili* explicitly condemns it in proposition n. 53: "*Constitutio organica Ecclesiae non est immutabilis; sed societas christiana perpetuae evolutioni, aeque societas humana, est obnoxia*" (Denzinger, n. 3453).

13. Vatican Council I, Sess. III, Dogmatic Constitution *Dei Filius* (Denzinger, n. 3008).

Saviour, for the exaltation of the Catholic religion and for the salvation of the Christian people, with the approval of the Sacred Council, we teach and define as a divinely revealed dogma that when the Roman Pontiff speaks *ex cathedra,* that is, when, in the exercise of his office as shepherd and teacher of all Christians, in virtue of his supreme apostolic authority, he defines a doctrine concerning faith or morals to be held by the whole Church, he possesses, by the divine assistance promised to him in blessed Peter, that infallibility which the divine Redeemer willed His Church to enjoy in defining doctrine concerning faith or morals. Therefore, such definitions of the Roman Pontiff are of themselves, and not by the consent of the Church, irreformable.[14]

Gherardini notes:

Two infallibilities that are added or subtracted from each other are not at stake here, but one and the same charism, which has, in the Church, in the pope and in the bishops, collegially considered in communion with the pope, its lawful authority. This charism is expressed in a positive form, prior to and perhaps more significantly than in a negative form. It is at work when the Magisterium in announcing the Christian truth or settling eventual controversies remains faithful to the *depositum fidei* (1 Tim

14. Vatican Council I, Sess. IV, Constit. Dogm. *Pastor aeternus,* ch. IV (Denzinger, n. 3074): "Itaque Nos traditioni a fidei Christianae exordio perceptae fideliter inhaerendo, ad Dei Salvatoris nostri gloriam, religionis Catholicae exaltationem et Christianorum populorum salutem, sacro approbante Concilio, docemus et divinitus revelatum dogma esse definimus: Romanum Pontificem, cum ex Cathedra loquitur, id est, cum omnium Christianorum Pastoris et Doctoris munere fungens, pro suprema sua Apostolica auctoritate doctrinam de fide vel moribus ab universa Ecclesia tenendam definit, per assistentiam divinam, ipsi in beato Petro promissam, ea infallibilitate pollere, qua divinus Redemptor Ecclesiam suam in definienda doctrina de fide vel moribus instructam esse voluit; ideoque eiusmodi Romani Pontificis definitiones ex sese, non autem ex consensu Ecclesiae irreformabiles esse."

6:20; 2 Tim 1:4) or discovers new implications up until that moment unexplored.[15]

Theologians refer to the infallibility of the Church when they speak of an infallibility *in docendo* and an infallibility *in credendo*. The Church, in fact, is made up of a teaching part (*docens*) and a taught part (*discens*). It is only for the Church *docens* to teach revealed truth infallibly, whereas the Church *discens* receives and conserves this truth. However, alongside the infallibility in teaching, there is also the infallibility in believing, since neither the *corpus docendi*, invested with the power of teaching the entire Church, nor the universality of the faithful in believing, can fall into error. If, in fact, the flock of the faithful as a whole could fall into error, believing something to be of revelation which is not, the promise of divine assistance to the Church would be frustrated. St. Thomas Aquinas refers to the infallibility of the Church as a whole when he affirms: "it is impossible that the judgment of the universal Church is wrong in that which pertains to the Faith."[16]

The "Church learning" insofar as it believes encompasses not only the faithful but also priests, bishops, and the pope himself, since everyone is required to believe the truths revealed by God—superiors no less than inferiors. In the Church, there is, however, only one infallibility, in which all her members share in an organic and differentiated way: each one according to his ecclesial office. Individual Christians can err in matters of faith, even when they hold the highest ecclesiastical offices, but not the Church as such—she is always immaculate in her doctrine.

---

15. See "Msgr. Brunero Gherardini on Canonization and Infallibility," available at http://chiesaepostconcilio.blogspot.it/2012/02/mons-brunero-gherardini-su.html.

16. "*Certum est quod iudicium Ecclesiae universalis errare in his quae ad fidem pertinent, impossibile est*" (St. Thomas Aquinas, *Quodlibet*, 9, q. 8, a. 1).

This infallibility is expressed in the so-called *sensus fidelium*,[17] by which the entire people of God enjoys infallibility not only passively but also proactively, as often as they anticipate Church definitions or contribute towards making them clearer. For example, this occurred before the Council of Ephesus proclaimed the Virgin Mary as Mother of God. St. Cyril[18] and St. Celestine[19] attest that the Christian populace already acknowledged belief in the Divine Maternity as "*the faith that the Universal Church professes.*"[20] In the history of the Church, devotion to the Blessed Virgin was the field whereby the influence of the Holy Spirit on the faithful was manifested with *force majeure*.

The sensus fidei *in the history of the Church*

The first author to use the term *sensus fidei* seems to be Vincent of Lérins (who died around A.D. 445). In his *Commonitorium* he proposes as normative the Faith observed everywhere, always, and by all (*quod ubique, quod semper, quod ab omnibus creditum est*).[21] The first historical manifestation of the *sensus fidei*, however, may have been the Arian crisis, in which, according to the careful reconstruction by Blessed John Henry Newman (1801–1890),[22] the "Church teaching" appeared often uncertain and lost but the *sensus fidelium* preserved the integrity of the Faith, so much so that St. Hilary was able to say: "*Sanctiores sunt aures fideles populi labiis sacerdotum* [The ears of the faithful people are holier

17. Theology differentiates between *sensus fidei fidelis,* reflecting the personal attitude of the believer, and *sensus fidei fidelium,* reflecting the instinct of faith of the Church herself.

18. St. Cyril, *Epist. IV to Nestorius,* PG 77:47–50; *Epist. II ad Celestinum,* PG 77:84.

19. St. Celestine, *Epist. XII ad Cyrillum,* PG 77:92–99.

20. Ibid., 92–93.

21. Vincent of Lérins, *Commonitorium,* II, 5, PL 64:149.

22. John Henry Newman, *The Arians of the Fourth Century* (1833).

than the lips of the priests]."[23] Cardinal Newman writes: "There was a temporary suspension of the function of the *ecclesia docens*. The body of bishops failed in their confession of the faith. They spoke variously, one against another; there was nothing, after Nicaea, of firm, unvarying, consistent testimony, for nearly sixty years." During this period, he adds, "the Divine tradition committed to the infallible Church was proclaimed and maintained far more by the faithful than by the Episcopate."[24]

All of the great modern councils have referred to the *sensus fidei*. The Council of Trent made appeal repeatedly to the judgment of the entire Church in defending articles of the Catholic Faith. Its decree on the Sacrament of the Eucharist (1551), for example, invokes specifically "the general consensus of the Church," *universum Ecclesiae sensum*.[25] The Dominican Melchior Cano, who took part in the Council of Trent, in his treatise *De locis theologicis* for the first time treated the *sensus fidelium* extensively, defending against the Protestants the values Catholics recognize regarding the power of Tradition in theological argument.[26]

Furthermore, the dogmatic constitution *Pastor Aeternus* of the First Vatican Council, which defined the pope's infallible Magisterium, presupposed the *sensus fidei fidelium*. The original project of the Constitution *Supremi Pastoris*, which served as the basis for *Pastor Aeternus*, had a chapter on the infallibility of the Church (chapter IX).[27] Nonetheless, when the agenda for the day was discussed with the aim of

---

23. St. Hilary of Poitiers, *Contra Arianos vel Auxentium*, n. 6, PL 10:613.

24. John Henry Newman, *On Consulting the Faithful in Matters of Doctrine* (Geoffrey Chapman, London 1961), 75, 77.

25. Council of Trent, Sess. XIII, *Decretum de ss. Eucharistia* (Denzinger, n. 1637).

26. Melchior Cano, *De locis theologicis*, ed. Juan Belda Plans (Biblioteca de Autores Cristianos, Madrid 2006), Bk. IV, ch. 3.

27. Mansi 51:542–3.

addressing the question of pontifical infallibility, the discussion of this principle was adjourned and never taken up again. In his final *relatio*, Monsignor Gasser cites the example of the Immaculate Conception to show that the pope deemed consultation with the Church necessary before reaching the definition of the dogma. The research of Father Giovanni Perrone (1794–1876) on the patristic conception of the *sensus fidelium* had a strong influence on Pope Pius IX's decision to proceed with the definition of the dogma of the Immaculate Conception.[28] In the apostolic constitution that contains this dogmatic definition, *Ineffabilis Deus* (1854), Pius IX uses the language of Perrone to describe the concordant testimony of the bishops and the faithful.[29]

Like Pius IX, so also Pope Pius XII before defining the dogma of the bodily Assumption of Mary Most Holy wanted to consult the bishops of the entire world, who, besides voicing their opinion, had to testify to the devotion of their faithful.[30] In those years, the *sensus fidei* was the object of some important studies, in particular those by Franciscan Father Carlo Balić and the Redemptorist Clément Dillenschneider, the Dominican Claudio García Extremeño, and the Servite Tommaso Maria Bartolomei.[31]

The Second Vatican Council also dealt with the *sensus fidei* or *communis fidelium sensus*. In particular, section 12 of *Lumen Gentium* asserts:

---

28. Giovanni Perrone, *De Immaculato B. V. Maria Conceptu. An dogmatico decreto definiri possit, disquisitio theologica* (Marini, Rome 1847), 139, 143–45.

29. Cf. Pius IX, Apostolic Letter *Ineffabilis Deus*, of December 8, 1854, in *Pii IX Acta* 1 (1854), col. 597; Pius XII, Apostolic Constitution *Munificentissimus Deus* of November 1, 1950, in AAS 42 (1950), 753–54.

30. Cf. Pius XII's Letter *Deiparae Virginis* of May 1, 1946, in AAS 42 (1950), 728 ff.

31. Cf. Carlo Balić, O.F.M., *Il senso cristiano e il progresso del dogma*, in *Gregorianum* XXXIII.1 (1952), 106–34; Clément Dillenschneider, *Le sens de la foi et le progrès dogmatique du mystère marial* (Pontificia Academia

The entire body of the faithful, anointed as they are by the Holy One, cannot err in matters of belief. They manifest this special property by means of the whole people's supernatural discernment in matters of faith when "from the Bishops down to the last of the lay faithful" they show universal agreement in matters of faith and morals. That discernment in matters of faith is aroused and sustained by the Spirit of truth. It is exercised under the guidance of the sacred teaching authority, in faithful and respectful obedience to which the people of God accepts that which is not just the word of men but truly the word of God. Through it, the people of God adheres unwaveringly to the faith given once and for all to the saints, penetrates it more deeply with right thinking, and applies it more fully to life.

The fact that at times progressives have used this passage to contest the ecclesiastical authorities does not mean that it is false and that it cannot be understood, like many other passages from the council, in conformity with Tradition. It should be noted, moreover, that in the modern age the doctrine of the *sensus fidei* has been explored mainly by great theologians of the Roman School, such as Fathers Giovanni Perrone (1794–1876) and Matthias Joseph Scheeben (1836–1888) and Cardinals Johannes Baptiste Franzelin (1816–1886) and Louis Billot (1846–1931).[32] Cardinal Franzelin, in particular, underlines the role of the Holy Spirit in forming and maintaining the *conscientia fidei communis* of the Christian people, and like Melchior Cano he judges the *sensus fidelium*

Mariana Internationalis, Rome 1954); T.M. Bartolomei, *L'influsso del "Senso della Fede" nell'esplicitazione del Dogma dell'Immacolata Concezione della Beata Vergine degna Madre di Dio,* in *Marianum* 25 (1963), 297 ff.; Claudio García Extremeño, O.P., *El sentido de la fe criterio de tradición,* in *La Ciencia Tomista* 87 (1960), 569–605.

32. Walter Kasper, *Die Lehre von der Tradition in der Römischen Schule* (Herder, Friburg 1962), above all 94–102.

to be one of the organs of Tradition, of which it is a faithful echo.[33] I am reminded of Monsignor Gherardini, the latest brilliant exponent of the Roman School, who gave me a gift in the 1980's of a study dedicated to the *sensus fidei* by Don Jesús Sancho Bielsa.[34] There are other authors belonging to the same Opus Dei school who have given ample treatment to the *sensus fidei*, like the theologians Fernando Ocáriz and Antonio Blanco.[35]

In any event, throughout history the *sensus fidei* has been made manifest in the minds and hearts of ordinary laypeople before being described by theologians, as Benedict XVI recalled with these words:

> Important theologians like Duns Scotus enriched what the People of God already spontaneously believed about the Blessed Virgin and expressed in acts of devotion, in the arts and in Christian life in general with the specific contribution of their thought.... This is all thanks to that supernatural *sensus fidei*, namely, that capacity infused by the Holy Spirit that qualifies us to embrace the reality of the faith with humility of heart and mind.... May theologians always be ready to listen to this source of faith and

33. Cf. Jean-Baptiste Franzelin, *De divina Traditione et Scriptura* (1870), tr. and annotated by Abbé J.-M. Gleize as *La Tradition* (Courrier de Rome, Condé sur Noireau 2009), theses XI and XII, 131–96.

34. Jesús Sancho Bielsa, *Infalibilidad del pueblo de Dios. "Sensus fidei" e infalibilidad orgánica de la Iglesia en la constitución "Lumen Gentium" del Concilio Vaticano II* (Universidad de Navarra, Pamplona 1979); cf. Dario Vitali, *Sensus fidelium. Una funzione ecclesiale di intelligenza della fede* [*an ecclesial function of intelligence of the faith*] (Morcelliana, Brescia 1993); Christoph Ohly, *Sensus fidei fidelium* (EOS Verlag, St. Ottilien 1999); Gerardo Albano, *Il sensus fidelium. La partecipazione del popolo di Dio alla funzione profetica della Chiesa* (Pontificia Facoltà Teologica dell'Italia Meridionale [extract from doctoral dissertation], Naples 2008).

35. Fernando Ocáriz and Antonio Blanco, *Rivelazione, fede e credibilità. Corso di teologia fondamentale* (Edizioni Università della Santa Croce, Rome 2001).

retain the humility and simplicity of children! I mentioned this a few months ago saying: "There have been great scholars, great experts, great theologians, teachers of faith who have taught us many things. They have gone into the details of Sacred Scripture . . . but have been unable to see the mystery itself, its central nucleus. . . . The essential has remained hidden! . . . On the other hand, in our time there have also been 'little ones' who have understood this mystery. Let us think of St. Bernadette Soubirous; of St. Thérèse of Lisieux, with her new interpretation of the Bible that is 'non-scientific' but goes to the heart of Sacred Scripture."[36]

The nature of the sensus fidei *according to the teaching of theologians*

In 2014, the International Theological Commission, presided over by Cardinal Gerhard Ludwig Müller, Prefect of the Congregation for the Doctrine of the Faith, published a study entitled *The* Sensus Fidei *in the Life of the Church*, which was interesting above all for its references to St. Thomas Aquinas.[37] In these pages it is made clear that, unlike theology, which can be described as a *scientia fidei*, the *sensus fidei* is not a reflexive, conceptual knowledge of the mysteries of the Faith, but a spontaneous intuition, with which the believer adheres to the true Faith or rejects what opposes it.[38] It therefore derives from the Faith and is a property thereof.[39] It is compared to an instinct since it is a type of spontaneous intuition that comes from the innateness (connaturality) the

36. Benedict XVI, Audience of July 7, 2010, in *Insegnamenti* VI (2010), 30–31, citing his Homily for the Holy Mass with Members of the International Theological Commission, December 1, 2009, in *Insegnamenti* V. 2 (Libreria Editrice Vatican, Vatican City 2009), 634.

37. International Theological Commission, *The* Sensus Fidei *in the Life of the Church* (Libreria Editrice Vaticana, Vatican City, 2014).

38. Ibid., n. 54.

39. Ibid., n. 49.

virtue of faith establishes between the believing subject and the object of the authentic Faith. The theologians Ocáriz and Blanco define it as the

> capacity of the believer not only to believe what is presented to him by the Church as a truth of the Faith, but also and above all the facility of discerning, as if by instinct, what is in agreement with the Faith from what is not, and also the facility of drawing greater in-depth conclusions from the truths taught by the Magisterium, not by way of theological reasoning, but spontaneously, through a sort of innate (connatural) knowledge. The virtue of faith (*habitus fidei*) produces in fact an innateness (connaturality) of the human spirit with revealed mysteries, so that the supernatural truth attracts the intellect.[40]

The doctrine of knowledge *per quandam connaturalitatem* is a form of interior intelligence that springs from the faith as *instinctus* or *lumen fidei*: St. Thomas Aquinas explains it in the *Summa Theologiae*, when he asserts:

> Rectitude of judgment is twofold: first, on account of perfect use of reason; secondly, on account of a certain connaturality with the matter about which one has to judge. Thus, about matters of chastity, a man after inquiring with his reason forms a right judgement, if he has learnt the science of morals, while he who has the habit of chastity judges of such matters by a kind of connaturality.[41]

The reason is that the virtuous man has a stable disposition (*habitus*) in exercising a certain type of behavior. The chaste man loves instinctively what is pure and in a likewise immediate manner experiences a repugnance for what is

---

40. F. Ocáriz and A. Blanco, *Revelation, Faith and Credibility*, 84.
41. St. Thomas Aquinas, *Summa Theologiae*, II-IIae, q. 45, a. 2. See also José Miguel Pero-Sanz, *El conocimiento por connaturalidad* (Eunsa, Pamplona 1964).

turbid and impure. This "spiritual instinct" allows him to discern how to behave in the most difficult situations and thus resolve in practice problems that for moralists can remain abstract. "The *habitus* of faith," explains the Angelic Doctor, "possesses a capacity whereby, thanks to it, the believer is prevented from giving assent to what is contrary to the faith, just as chastity gives protection with regard to whatever is contrary to chastity."[42] Thus, in agreement with the connaturality that comes to him from this habit (*habitus*), "man adheres to the truths of the faith and not to the contrary errors, through the light of the faith infused in him by God."[43]

The supernatural capacity that the believer has in perceiving, penetrating, and applying to his life the revealed truth comes from the Holy Spirit. St. Thomas takes as a starting point the fact that the universal Church is governed by the Holy Spirit, who, as Jesus Christ promised, "will teach [her] the entire truth" (Jn 16:13).[44] "Showing the truth," says the Angelic Doctor, "is a property of the Holy Spirit, because it is love that brings about the revelation of secrets."[45]

This sense of the faith exists in all believers, including sinners, even if he who is in a state of grace has a deeper and more intense insight into the dogmas of faith than he who is in sin; and among those who are in a state of grace the insight is proportionate to the level of sanctity. Such insight in fact is an illumination that comes from the grace of the faith and the gifts of the Holy Spirit in the soul, especially those of understanding, knowledge, and wisdom.[46]

This Christian sense has nothing whatever to do with

---

42. St. Thomas Aquinas, *De Veritate*, q. 14, a. 10, ad 10.

43. *Summa Theologiae*, II-IIae, q. 2, a. 3, ad 2.

44. *Summa Theologiae*, II-IIae, q. 1, a. 9.

45. *Expositio super Ioannis Evangelium*, c. 14, lec. 4.

46. Tommaso M. Bartolomei, *Natura, realtà, genesi e valore del "Sensus fidei*," 270.

"religious sentiment" in the modernist sense condemned in the encyclical *Pascendi* of St. Pius X, and even less so with that *facultas appetendi et affectandi* [faculty of desire and affection] of which the encyclical *Humani Generis* of Pius XII[47] makes mention. The *sensus fidei*, in fact, is not a product of the sensibilities, but of faith, grace, and the gifts of the Holy Spirit that enlighten the intellect and move the will.[48]

The Holy Spirit Who dwells in the faithful does not remain inactive. He lives in the soul to illuminate it like the sun. The inspirations of the Holy Spirit are a reality that can accompany the ordinary life of every Christian faithful to the action of grace. The divine inspiration of the Holy Spirit, as Father Arnaldo Maria Lanz, S.J., explains, must not be confused with interior revelations and locutions, which communicate new ideas through an extraordinary influence, but it is a divine "instinct" that helps us know and act better under the influence of God.[49] Writes Father Balić:

> Now, this Spirit of the Seven Gifts Who dwells in us, not as in the midst of ruins, but as in a temple (1 Cor 3:16–17; 6:19), is the Spirit of Pentecost; He is the Spirit of Truth (Jn 14:17) whose special mission consists in revealing to the world the full substance of Christ and all the wonders the Son of God had kept hidden or had not completely and clearly revealed.[50]

Thanks to the *sensus fidei* the believer perceives the truths preserved in the revealed deposit of faith. Thus the promise of St. John is fulfilled: "But you have the unction from the Holy One and know all things" (1 Jn 2:20), on which Bishop Rich-

47. Pius XII, Encyclical *Humani Generis* of August 12, 1950, in AAS 42 (1950), 574–75.

48. C. Balić, *Il senso cristiano*, 113–14.

49. Arnaldo Maria Lanz, "Ispirazione divina," in *Enciclopedia cattolica*, 7:326–27.

50. Balić, *Il senso cristiano*, 110.

ard Challoner comments: "that is, grace and wisdom from the Holy Ghost."

Sensus fidei, *Magisterium, and Tradition*

Father Balić also calls the *sensus fidei* "Catholic common sense" or "Christian sense" (*sensus christianus*).[51] In philosophy, ordinary common sense is the intelligence and natural light with which men are normally endowed: a quality that permits the understanding of the notions of good and evil, true and false, beauty and ugliness.[52] "Catholic common sense" is the supernatural light received by the Christian at Baptism and Confirmation. These sacraments infuse in us the capacity to adhere to the truths of the faith through supernatural instinct, even when we lack an aptitude for theological reasoning.

In the same way that common sense is measured by the objectivity of the real, the *sensus fidei* is measured by the objective rule of the truths of the Faith contained in the Church's Tradition. The proximate rule of the Faith is the infallible Magisterium of the Church, which is the domain only of those who, by Christ's will, have the right and the office to teach: the Apostles and their successors. The mass of the faithful has no part in this official teaching and is limited to receiving it. "They would err, however," writes Father Balić,

> who think that this mass is in a merely passive and mechanical state in regard to this doctrine. And in fact the faith of the laity, like the doctrine of the shepherds, is sustained by the influence of the Holy Spirit, and the faithful by their Christian sense and profession of Faith contribute

51. Balić, *Il senso cristiano*, 112–13.

52. Réginald Garrigou-Lagrange, O.P., *Le sens commun: la philosophie de l'être et les formules dogmatiques* (Nouvelle Librairie Nationale, Paris 1922); Msgr. Antonio Livi, *Filosofia del senso commune. Logica della scienza e della fede* (Edizioni Leonardo da Vinci, Rome 2010).

to the exposition, publication, manifestation, and testimony of the Christian truth.[53]

The faithful, although they have no mission to teach, have the function of preserving and propagating their faith. The theologians Ocáriz and Blanco write, citing Cardinal Franzelin: "The infallibility of the '*sensus fidei*' manifested by the '*consensus fidelium*' exists even when it refers to a truth not yet infallibly taught by the Magisterium. In this case the '*consensus fidelium*' is a certain criterion of truth since it is a criterion '*divinae traditionis*,'"[54] *sub ductu magisterii*, under the guidance of the Magisterium. The Magisterium nevertheless is not the source of Revelation, as opposed to Scripture and Tradition, which together constitute the "remote rule" of the faith and with which the Magisterium is nourished. In this sense Cardinal Franzelin, citing St. Irenæus, defines Tradition as the "immutable rule of truth," since it is nothing other than the Church's integral doctrine that comes to us from the successors of the Apostles with the assistance of the Holy Spirit.[55]

Cardinal Franzelin cites St. Athanasius, St. Epiphanius, and St. Hilary in support of his thesis. The latter speaks of the "conscience of the common faith," opposed to the "impious intelligence" of the heretics.[56] St. Augustine defines "the rule of faith" as that "faith with which we have been nourished"[57] and designates it as an objective truth found in the Church, where we have received it.[58] Cardinal Billot defines Tradition as "the rule of faith anterior to all the others," a rule of faith not only remote but also close and immediate,

---

53. Balić, *Il senso cristiano*, 125–26.

54. F. Ocáriz and A. Blanco, *Revelation,* 85.

55. Franzelin, *La Tradition*, n. 184, p. 134.

56. Ibid., n. 188, p. 136.

57. St. Augustine, *Commentary on the Gospel of St. John*, tract. 18, n. 1, in PL 35:1536.

58. Franzelin, *La Tradition*, n. 192, p. 138.

depending on the point of view being proposed to us.[59] Monsignor Brunero Gherardini offers this definition: "Tradition is the official transmission on the part of the Church and her organs, which are divinely instituted, and infallibly assisted by the Holy Spirit, of Divine Revelation in [the] spatial-temporal dimension."[60]

It should be remembered that the Church is the Mystical Body of which Christ is the Head, the Holy Spirit the Soul, and all the faithful, from the pope down to the last baptized person, are the members. The Church as a whole, however, should not be confused with the churchmen that form her. The Church is impeccable, infallible, indefectible. Churchmen, individually taken, are not, with the exception of the pope or a council gathered under his name to define solemnly a question of faith, whose task, under the proper conditions, has the privilege of infallibility. In the absence of the required conditions, the pope or a council can err, and those who consider them always infallible fall into the error of papolatry (or councilolatry) that leads to wrongfully attributing to the Church *per se* a responsibility for the many failures, scandals, and errors of some popes who have governed her.[61]

The International Theological Commission has stated: "Alerted by their *sensus fidei*, individual believers may deny assent even to the teaching of legitimate pastors if they do not recognise in that teaching the voice of Christ, the Good

59. Louis Billot, S.J., *De immutabilitate traditionis* (1907); tr. with footnotes of Abbé J.-M. Gleize, *Tradition et modernisme. De l'immuable tradition, contre la nouvelle hérésie de l'évolutionnisme* (Courrier de Rome, Villegenon 2007), 32, 37.

60. B. Gherardini, *Quaecumque dixero vobis* (Lindau, Turin 2011), 170.

61. See P. Enrico Zoffoli, *La vera Chiesa di Cristo* (Pro manuscripto, Roma 1990), *Chiesa e uomini di Chiesa. Apologetica a rovescio* (Edizioni Segno, Udine 1994), and *Potere e obbedienza nella Chiesa* (Maurizio Minchella Editore, Rome 1996).

Shepherd."[62] In fact, as the Apostle John recalls, "the sheep follow him [the Good Shepherd] because they know his voice. But a stranger they follow not, but fly from him, because they know not the voice of strangers" (Jn 10: 4–5).

For St. Thomas Aquinas, even if a believer lacks theological competence, he can and actually must resist—by virtue of his *sensus fidei*—his bishop, if the latter is preaching heterodox things.[63] Again St. Thomas teaches that in extreme cases it is licit and actually right and proper to resist publicly even a papal decision, as St. Paul resisted St. Peter to his face: "Hence Paul, who was Peter's subject, rebuked him in public, on account of the imminent danger of scandal concerning the faith, and, as the gloss of Augustine says, 'Peter gave an example to superiors, that if at any time they should happen to stray from the straight path, they should not disdain to be reproved by their subjects' (Gal 2:14)."[64]

The *sensus fidei* can induce the faithful, in some cases, to refuse their assent to some ecclesiastical documents and place themselves, before the supreme authority, in a situation of resistance and apparent disobedience. The disobedience is only apparent since in these cases of legitimate resistance the evangelical principle that one must obey God rather than men prevails (Acts 5: 29).[65]

---

62. International Theological Commission, *The* Sensus Fidei *in the Life of the Church*, n. 63.

63. St. Thomas Aquinas, *In* 3 *Sent.*, d. 25, q. 2, a. 1, sol. 2, ad 3.

64. *Summa Theologiae*, II-II, q. 33, a. 4, ad 2.

65. See, for example, Plinio Corrêa de Oliveira's manifesto, *A política de distensão do Vaticano com os governos comunistas. Para a TFP: omitir-se? ou resistir?* (in *Catolicismo*, n. 280 [April 1974], 4–5, published in 57 newspapers of 11 countries), and the letter sent on November 21, 1983 by Archbishop Marcel Lefebvre and Bishop Antonio de Castro Mayer to Pope John Paul II regarding some errors in the new Code of Canon Law and the ceremonies performed on occasion of the five-hundredth anniversary of Luther (Bernard Tissier de Mallerais, *Marcel Lefebvre. Une vie* [Clovis, Etampes 2002], 559–60).

Legitimate "disobedience" to an order unjust in itself, in the area of faith and morals, may be required—in particular cases—even to the point of publicly resisting the Supreme Pontiff. Arnaldo Xavier da Silveira, in a study dedicated to public resistance to the decisions of ecclesiastical authority,[66] demonstrated this very clearly by citing quotations from the saints, doctors of the Church, illustrious theologians, and canon lawyers.

The Code of Canon Law now in force, from canon 208 to canon 223 (under the title *De omnium Christifidelium obligationibus et iuribus*), outlines the status common to all the faithful and ascribes to the laity the responsibility of intervening in the crises of the Church. Canon 212 says:

> According to the knowledge, competence, and prestige they possess, the faithful have the right and even at times the duty to manifest to the sacred pastors their opinion on matters that pertain to the good of the Church and to make their opinion known to the rest of the Christian faithful, without prejudice to the integrity of faith and morals, with reverence toward their pastors, and attentive to common advantage and the dignity of persons.

Rules to discern and foster the sensus fidei

What is the criterion for discerning and fostering the authentic *sensus fidei*? We have said many times that the *sensus fidei* is in no way a subjective sentiment, it is not the free examination of the Protestants, it is not a charismatic experience. It is a supernatural instinct rooted in the objective faith of the Church expressed by her Magisterium and Tradition.

---

66. A. Xavier da Silveira, "Resistenza pubblica a delle decisioni dell' autorità ecclesiastica," in *Ipotesi teologica di un Papa eretico*, 141–56. Cf. also idem, *Can Documents of the Magisterium of the Church Contain Errors?* (The American Society for the Defense of Tradition, Family and Property, Spring Grove [PA] 2015).

The Magisterium can be understood in two senses: as an act of the ecclesiastical authority that teaches a truth (subjective Magisterium) or as an object believed, a set of truths taught (objective Magisterium). In the first case the Magisterium is a function exercised by the ecclesiastical authority to teach revealed Truths, in the second case it is an objective deposit of truth that coincides with Tradition.

The *sensus fidei* plays a decisive role during times of crisis in which an evident contradiction between the subjective Magisterium and the objective one is created, between the authorities that teach and the truths of the Faith they must guard and transmit. The *sensus fidei* induces the believer to reject any ambiguity or falsification of the truth, leaning on the immutable Tradition of the Church, which does not oppose the Magisterium but includes it.

The ultimate rule of the faith is not the contemporary "living" Magisterium, which actually often seems to intend to be vague and non-defining, but Tradition, or rather the objective and perennial Magisterium, which constitutes, along with Holy Scripture, one of the two sources of the Word of God. Ordinarily the Magisterium is the proximate rule of faith, inasmuch as it transmits and applies infallible truths contained in the deposit of Revelation; but in the case of a contrast between the novelties proposed by the subjective or "living" Magisterium and Tradition, the primacy can only be given to Tradition, for one simple motive: Tradition, which is the "living" Magisterium in its universality and continuity, is in itself infallible, whereas the so-called "living" Magisterium, meant as the current preaching of the ecclesiastical hierarchy, is only so in determinate conditions. Tradition in fact is always divinely assisted; the Magisterium is so only when it is expressed in an extraordinary way, or when, in its ordinary form, it teaches with continuity *over time* a truth of faith and morals. The fact that the ordinary Magisterium cannot constantly teach a truth contrary to the faith does not exclude that this same Magisterium may fall *per accidens* into error, when the teaching is circumscribed in space and time and is not expressed in an extraordinary manner.[67]

This does not mean in any way that the dogmatic truth must be the result of the sentiment of laypeople and that nothing can be defined without first hearing the opinion of the universal Church, as if the Magisterium were simply a revealer of the faith of the people, quasi-regulated by them in its magisterial function.[68] It means, however, as Padre Garcia Extremeño asserts, that the Magisterium cannot propose anything infallibly to the Church if it is not contained in Tradition, which is the supreme *regula fidei* of the Church.[69]

Tradition is maintained and transmitted by the Church, not only through the Magisterium, but through all the faithful, "from the bishops down to the laity,"[70] as the famous formula by St. Augustine cited in *Lumen Gentium* 12 expresses. The doctor from Hippo makes an appeal in particular to "the people of the faith,"[71] who do not exercise a Magisterium but on the basis of their *sensus fidei* guarantee the continuity of the transmission of Truth.

It is evident from what we have said that the *sensus fidei*, like the act of faith for that matter, has a rational foundation. When the *sensus fidei* points out a contrast between some

---

67. R. de Mattei, *Apologia della Tradizione* (Lindau, Turin 2011), 146–47.

68. The decree *Lamentabili*, n. 6, condemns the modernist proposition according to which "*In definiendis veritatibus ita collaborant discens et docens Ecclesia, ut docenti Ecclesiae nihil supersit, nisi communes discentis opinationes sancire*" (Denzinger, n. 3406): "In defining the truth the 'Church learning' and the 'Church teaching' collaborate in such a way in defining truths that it only remains for the 'Church teaching' to sanction the opinions of the 'Church learning.'"

69. C. García Extremeño, O.P., *El sentido de la fe criterio de tradición*, 602.

70. St. Augustine, *De praedestinatione sanctorum*, 14, 27, in PL 44:980.

71. St. Augustine, *Contra secundam Iuliani responsionem imperfectum opus*, II/1.

expressions of the current Magisterium and the Tradition of the Church, its foundation is not the theological competence of the believer, but the good use of logic, illuminated by grace. In this sense, the principle of non-contradiction constitutes a fundamental criterion of verification of the act of faith, as is the case in every intellectual act.[72] Everything that appears irrational and contradictory repels the *sensus fidei*. The faith is based on reason, since the act of faith by its very nature is an act of the intellectual faculties. "The noblest act of the intellect that a man can make in this mortal life is most certainly the act of faith," observes Father Christian Pesch (1835–1925),[73] who explains that the act of faith cannot be freed from the intellect, by replacing the essence of the faith with an irrational abandonment to God, in the Lutheran manner. He who denies the evidence of reason falls into fideism, which has nothing whatever to do with the true Faith.

Furthermore, the adhesion of the conscience to the principles of faith or morals is always rational. The conscience is in fact the judgment of the practical intellect, which, grounded in the light of the primary rational principles, evaluates the morality of our acts in their concrete singularity.[74] Our conscience does not have its objective rule in the person of the pope or a bishop, but in the divine and natural law, which the supreme authorities of the Church have the task of transmitting and defending. Therefore, as Cardinal Newman says, "conscience is the aboriginal vicar of Christ."[75] Faced with a proposition that contradicts faith or morals, we have the moral duty to follow our conscience, which opposes it. Nobody can be obliged to adhere to a

---

72. J.-M. Gleize, "Magistère et foi," in *Courrier de Rome*, n. 344 (2011), 3.

73. P. Cristiano Pesch, S.J., *Il dovere della fede* (F. Pustet, Rome 1910), 41.

74. Ramon Garcia de Haro, *La vita cristiana. Corso di teologia morale fondamentale* (Ares, Milan 1995), 377–78.

75. J.H. Newman, *Letter to the Duke of Norfolk*, sec. 5.

principle he judges false, nor commit an act that in conscience he judges unjust.

The faith that is illuminated by grace nurtures, moreover, the interior life of the believer. Without an interior life, one does not obtain the help that comes from grace, which has its only source in Jesus Christ. The pope, the vicar of Christ but not His successor, is not in himself a source of divine grace. Regarding this, Father Roger Calmel writes:

> It is necessary that our interior life be directed not to the pope, but to Jesus Christ. Our interior life, which evidently includes the truths of Revelation about the pope, must be directed purely to the High Priest, Our God and Savior Jesus Christ, in order to triumph over the scandals that come to the Church from the pope.[76]

God acts in history as the exemplary cause of the universe in His own attribute of Divine Wisdom. The *sensus fidei* is nurtured also in this exemplarity, by imitating the models the history of the Church has offered us. The first and most excellent model to be imitated is Jesus Christ, Wisdom Incarnate, above all in the Agony in Gethsemane; the second model to be imitated is the Blessed Virgin, above all on Holy Saturday when her faith summed up that of the Church: "*apostolis fugientibus, in Passione Domini fides Ecclesiae in beatissima Virgine sola remansit* [the Apostles having fled, during the Passion of the Lord the faith of the Church remained in the Most Blessed Virgin alone];"[77] the examples of the Saints like St. Athanasius, St. Bruno of Segni, St. Peter Damian, St. Bridget, St. Catherine, and St. Louis-Marie Grignion de Montfort, who were illuminated by the Holy Spirit during dramatic times in

---

76. R. T. Calmel, O.P., *Breve apologia della Chiesa di sempre*, tr. Edizioni Ichthys (Albano Laziale, Rome 2007), 121.

77. Carolus Binder, *Thesis, in Passione Domini Fidem Ecclesiae in Beatissima Virgine sola remansisse, iuxta doctrinam Medi Aevii et recentioris aetate*, in *Maria et Ecclesia. Acta Congressus Mariologici Lourdes*, vol. III (Academia Mariana Internationalis, Rome 1959), 389–487.

Church history. The Saints, writes St. Bernard of Clairvaux, appear on earth to be our models and are taken to heaven to be our patrons.[78] And today we need models and patrons more than ever.

The *sensus fidei*, in the end, has to be transformed into that confidence which, as Father Saint-Laurent states, citing St. Thomas, represents the summit of the theological virtues of faith and hope.[79] The problems we are faced with, like the presence of heresies in pontifical documents and the hypothesis of a heretic pope, are of enormous importance. We do not claim to resolve them at a conference, in an article, or in a book or a conversation. But neither can we recoil from the evidence of the facts. The questions of a heretic pope and heretical magisterial documents can give rise to distress of a psychological more than a theological order, when it passes from the abstract level to the concrete. At times we are terrified when faced with the consequences that can open up in the life of the Church as well as each one of us at the idea of a pope *a fide devius* [who has deviated from the faith]. But denying the evidence for fear of the consequences would show a lack of that confidence in Divine Providence which will allow us to resolve these problems one moment at a time, by abandoning ourselves to the action of the Holy Spirit in our souls.

Sufficit diei malitia sua: sufficient for the day is the evil thereof (Mt 6:34). We need not expect to resolve tomorrow's problems today without the grace that tomorrow brings. All of the Saints lived in this spirit of abandonment, fulfilling the Divine Will in the way it was made manifest to them

78. St. Bernard of Clairvaux, *In Natalis S. Victoris*, s. 2, 1 in PL 183:174, quoted in Msgr Antonio Piolanti, *Il mistero della comunione dei santi nella rivelazione e nella teologia* (Desclée, Rome 1957), 786.

79. St. Thomas Aquinas, *Summa Theologiae*, II-II, q. 129, art. 6, ad 3. Cf. Thomas de Saint Laurent, *Il libro della fiducia* (Ed. Fiducia, Rome 1991).

moment by moment, without allowing themselves to worry about the future. "Their secret," writes Father Garrigou-Lagrange, "was living moment by moment what the divine action wanted to make of them."[80]

It will be the Blessed Virgin Mary, the destroyer of all heresies, who will show us the way to continue professing the true faith and resist evil actively in ways that the situation will impose on us. We are not infallible, and the pope is so only under determinate conditions. But the divine promise is infallible: "*Ego vobiscum sum omnibus diebus usque ad consummationem saeculi*" (Mt 28:20). "Behold I am with you all days, even to the consummation of the world." This is the source of our unshakeable confidence.

80. Réginald Garrigou-Lagrange, O.P., *La Providence et la confiance en Dieu* (Les Editions Militia, Montréal 1953), 256.

Tu Es Petrus:
True Devotion to the
Chair of Saint Peter[1]

I T IS A GREAT JOY for me to participate in this gathering, not only because of the very interesting talks, but also because it is an opportunity to pay homage to the memory of a dear friend, John Vennari, to whom I dedicate my talk.

We find ourselves before one of the most critical moments that the Church has ever experienced in her history, but I am convinced that true devotion to the Chair of Saint Peter can offer us the weapons to come out of this crisis victorious.

True devotion. Because there is also false devotion to the Chair of Peter, just as—according to Saint Louis-Marie Grignion de Montfort—there is a true and a false devotion to the Most Blessed Virgin Mary.

The promise of Our Lord to Simon Peter in the city of Caesarea Philippi is clear: "*Tu es Petrus, et super hanc petram aedificabo Ecclesiam meam, et portae inferi non praevalebunt adversus eam*: Thou art Peter; and upon this rock I will build my church, and the gates of hell shall not prevail against it" (Mt 16:15–19). The primacy of Peter constitutes the bedrock on which Jesus Christ instituted His Church, and on which she will remain solid until the end of time. The promise of the Church's victory, however, is also the announcement of a

---

1. A lecture given at the *Catholic Family News* Conference "Weapons of Our Warfare," April 7, 2018, Deerfield, Illinois, USA.

war: a war that will be waged by hell against the Church until the end of time. At the center of this fierce war is the papacy. The enemies of the Church throughout the course of history have always sought to destroy the primacy of Peter, because they have understood that it comprises the visible foundation of the Mystical Body—the *visible* foundation, because the Church has a primary and invisible foundation, Jesus Christ, of Whom Peter is the Vicar.

True devotion to the Chair of Peter is, under this aspect, devotion to the visibility of the Church, and constitutes, as Father Faber observers, an essential part of the Christian spiritual life.[2]

Attacks against the papacy throughout history

One of the most violent attacks endured by the papacy throughout history took place in the years that preceded the French Revolution, under the pontificate of Pope Pius VI (r. 1775–1799), Gianangelo Braschi. In Germany, the theologian Johann Nikolaus von Hontheim, known by the pseudonym Justinus Febronius, denied the primacy of Peter and supported an ecclesiastical organization in which the supreme power would be held by the collegiality of bishops. Febronius claimed that he did not wish to challenge the pope but the centralized power of the Roman Curia, which he wanted to counterpose with national or provincial episcopal synods. Pius VI condemned his theses with the decree *Super Soliditate Petrae* of November 28, 1786.

In Italy, analogous ideas were expressed by the Jansenist bishop of Pistoia, Scipione de' Ricci. In 1786, Scipione de' Ricci called a diocesan synod with the intention of reforming the Church, reducing the pope to being merely the min-

---

2. Frederick William Faber, *La devozione e fedeltà al Papa*, in AA. VV., *Il Papa nel pensiero degli scrittori religiosi e politici*, vol. II (*La Civiltà Cattolica*, Roma 1927), 231–38.

isterial head of the community of Christian pastors. Then
the French Revolution broke out, and Pius VI, with the letter
Quod Aliquantum of March 10, 1791, condemned the Civil
Constitution of the Clergy, which affirmed that the bishops
were independent of the pope, that priests were superior to
bishops, and that parish priests were to be elected by the
simple faithful. With the bull *Auctorem Fidei* of August 28,
1794, the ecclesiological errors of the Synod of Pistoia were
also condemned.[3]

Pius VI, however, was overwhelmed by the Revolution. In
1796 Bonaparte's fleet invaded the Italian peninsula and
occupied Rome, and on February 15, 1798, he proclaimed the
Roman Republic. The pope was arrested and brought to the
city of Valence in France, where he died on August 29, 1799,
worn out by his sufferings. The Revolution seemed to have
triumphed over the Church. The body of Pius VI was left
unburied for several months, after which it was brought to
the local cemetery in a trunk used as a casket for the poor,
on which was written "Citizen Gianangelo Braschi—whose
stage name was 'Pope.'" The municipality of Valence notified
the French Directory of the death of Pius VI, adding that the
last pope of history had been buried.

Ten years later, in 1809, the successor of Pius VI, Pius
VII—old and infirm—was also arrested, and after two years
of imprisonment in Savona was taken to Fontainebleau,
where he remained until the fall of Napoleon, forced to bow
to his will. Never before had the papacy appeared to the
world to be so weak. But ten years later, in 1819, Napoleon
was gone from the scene, and Pius VII had returned to the
papal throne, recognized as supreme moral authority by the
European sovereigns. In that year, 1819, the book *Du Pape*
[On the Pope] was published in Lyon, the masterpiece of
Count Joseph de Maistre—a work that would see hundreds

3. Denzinger, 2601–612.

of reprints, and anticipated the dogma of papal infallibility later defined by the First Vatican Council. The book *Du Pape* is considered as a manifesto of ultramontane or counter-revolutionary thought, which opposes itself to the Catholic liberalism of the nineteenth and twentieth centuries. Here today, I would like to be an echo of this school of Catholic thought, of which John Vennari was also an exponent.[4]

When the First Vatican Council opened in 1869, two parties clashed. On one side stood the ultramontane or counter-revolutionary Catholics, supported by Pius IX, who fought for the approbation of the dogmas of the primacy of Peter and papal infallibility. Among these were illustrious bishops, like Cardinal Henry Edward Manning, archbishop of Westminster; Bishop Louis Pie, bishop of Poitiers; and Bishop Konrad Martin, bishop of Paderborn, joined by the best theologians of the time, among them Fathers Giovanni Battista Franzelin, Joseph Kleutgen, and Henri Ramière. On the opposing side were the liberal Catholics headed by Monsignor Maret, dean of the theological faculty of Paris, and Ignaz von Döllinger, rector of the University of Munich.

The liberals, echoing the conciliarist and Gallican theses, held that the authority of the Church did not reside in the pontiff alone but in the pope united to the bishops, and judged the dogma of infallibility to be erroneous, or at least inopportune. On December 8, 1870, Pius IX defined the dogmas of the primacy of Peter and papal infallibility by means of the constitution *Pastor Aeternus.*[5] Today, these dogmas are for us a precious benchmark on which to base true devotion to the Chair of Peter.

---

4. For a synthesis of this line of thought, see Plinio Corrêa de Oliveira, *Revolution and Counter-Revolution* (The American Society for the Defense of Tradition, Family, Property, York [PA] 1993).

5. Denzinger, 3050–75.

The Second Vatican Council and the new conception of the papacy

Liberal Catholics were defeated by the First Vatican Council, but a century later they would become the protagonists and winners of Vatican II.

Gallicans, Jansenists, and Febronianists openly held that the structure of the Church has to be democratic, led from the bottom, by priests and bishops, of whom the pope would be only a representative. The constitution *Lumen Gentium*, promulgated on November 21, 1964 by Pope Paul VI and the fathers of the Second Vatican Council, was like all of the council documents an ambiguous one, which recognized these tendencies yet without bringing them to their logical conclusion.

The *Nota Explicativa Praevia* [preliminary explanatory note] desired by Paul VI to save the orthodoxy of the document was a compromise between the principle of the primacy of Peter and that of the collegiality of the bishops. What took place with *Lumen Gentium* also occurred with the conciliar constitution *Gaudium et Spes*, which placed on the same level the procreative and unitive ends of matrimony. Equality in nature does not exist. One of the two principles is destined to assert itself over the other. And as in the case of matrimony, the unitive principle has now prevailed over the procreative, so in the case of the constitution of the Church, the principle of collegiality is imposing itself on that of the primacy of the Roman Pontiff.

Synodality, collegiality, and *decentralization* are the words that today express the attempt to transform the monarchical and hierarchical constitution of the Church into a democratic and parliamentary structure. A programmatic "manifesto" of this new ecclesiology is the discourse given by Pope Francis on October 17, 2015, during the ceremony for the fiftieth anniversary of the institution of the Synod of Bishops. In that speech, Francis used the image of the "upside-down pyramid" to describe the "conversion" of the papacy already announced in the exhortation *Evangelii Gaudium* of 2013 (n. 32). It seems that Pope Bergoglio wants to replace the Roman-centric Church with a polycentric or multisided church, according to an image he often uses. A renewed papacy would then be conceived as a form of ministry at the service of the other churches, renouncing the juridical primacy or government of Peter.

In order to democratize the Church, the innovators seek to strip her of her institutional aspect and to reduce her to a purely sacramental dimension. It is the transition from a juridical Church to a sacramental Church, a Church of communion. What are the consequences? On a sacramental level, the pope, as a bishop, is equal to all other bishops. That which places him above all the bishops and confers upon him a supreme, full, and immediate power over the whole Church is his juridical office. The specific *munus* of the Supreme Pontiff does not consist in his power of orders, which he has in common with all bishops of the world, but in his power of jurisdiction, or of government, which distinguishes him from every other bishop. The office held by the pope does not represent a fourth level of Holy Orders following the diaconate, priesthood, and episcopacy. The Petrine ministry is not a sacrament but an office, because the pope is the visible vicar of Jesus Christ. The Sacrament-Church model dissolves the primacy of Peter, and with it the visibility of the Church.

The visibility of the Church

Jesus Christ entrusted the mission of governing to Peter, after the Resurrection, when He said: "Feed My lambs, feed My sheep" (Jn 21:15–17). With these words, Our Lord confirmed the promise made to the Prince of the Apostles at Caesarea Philippi and made him His visible Vicar on earth, with the powers of supreme head of the Church and universal pastor. True devotion to the Chair of Peter is not the worship of the man who occupies this *cathedra*, but the love and veneration for the mission that Jesus Christ gave to Peter and to his successors. This mission is a visible mission, perceptible to the senses, as explained by Leo XIII in the encyclical *Satis Cognitum* (1896) and Pius XII in his encyclical *Mystici Corporis Christi* (1943). Pius XII teaches that, like her Founder, the Church consists in a human element, visible and external, and a divine element, spiritual and invisible. She is a society, visible and spiritual, temporal and eternal at the same time, human for the members of which she is composed, and divine for her origin, her end, and her supernatural means. The Church has a first visibility because she is neither a spiritual current or a movement of ideas, but a true society endowed with a juridical structure; and a second visibility because she is a supernatural society recognizable by her external marks, by which she is always one, holy, Catholic, apostolic, and Roman. "The second visibility, namely, that of the [four] marks," as Cardinal Billot asserts, "includes the first visibility of the [human] society endowed with its hierarchy, although it surpasses it."[6]

The pope is he in whom this visibility of the Church is concentrated and condensed. This is the meaning of the phrase of Saint Ambrose: "*Ubi Petrus, ibi ecclesia* [Where Peter is, there is the Church],"[7] which presupposes a saying attributed to Saint Ignatius of Antioch: "*Ubi Christus, ibi ecclesia* [Where Christ is, there is the Church]."[8] There is no true Church outside of that founded by Jesus Christ, Who continues to guide and assist her invisibly, while her Vicar visibly governs her on earth.

Pius XII goes on to explain in *Mystici Corporis*:

---

6. Louis Billot, *De Ecclesia Christi*, I (Prati, Giachetti 1909), 49–51.
7. St. Ambrose, *Expositio in Psalmos*, 40.
8. St. Ignatius of Antioch, *Epistle to the Smyrnaeans*, 8, 2.

For Peter in view of his primacy is only Christ's Vicar; so that there is only one chief Head of this Body, namely Christ, who never ceases Himself to guide the Church invisibly, though at the same time He rules it visibly, through him who is His representative on earth. After His glorious Ascension into Heaven this Church rested not on Him alone, but on Peter, too, its visible foundation stone.

Today, there is a modernist infiltration inside the Church, but there are not two churches. This is the reason why Fr. Gleize judges that speaking of the "Conciliar Church" is inaccurate, affirming that two churches do not exist:

> There is Rome and the Church, the one Mystical Body of Christ, of which the visible head is the pope, Bishop of Rome and Vicar of Christ. But there are also bad tendencies that have been introduced into this Church because of the false ideas that are wreaking havoc in the minds of those who are in power in Rome.[9]

And this is also the reason for which we need to be careful of speaking of the "Bergoglian church," or of "the new Church." The Church today is occupied by churchmen who betray or deform the message of Christ, but it has not been replaced by another church. There is only one Catholic Church, in which today cohabitate in a confused and fragmentary way different and counterpoised theologies and philosophies. It is more correct to speak of a Bergoglian theology, of a Bergoglian philosophy, of Bergoglian morality, and, if one wishes, of a Bergoglian religion, without coming to the point of defining Pope Bergoglio, the cardinals, the Curia, and the bishops of the whole world as a "Bergoglian church." If we were to imagine that the pope, the cardinals, the Curia, and the world's bishops comprise as a whole a

9. Fr. Jean-Michel Gleize, FSSPX, *Angelus*, July 2013.

new Church, we would have to legitimately ask ourselves: "Where is the Church of Christ? Where is her social and supernatural visibility?"

And this is the principal argument against sedevacantism. But it is also an argument against that inflated traditionalism that, while not declaring the vacancy of the See of Peter, thinks itself able to kick the pope, cardinals, and bishops out of the Church and *de facto* reduces the Mystical Body of Christ to a purely spiritual and invisible reality.

The error of papolatry

The Church, as a visible society, needs a visible hierarchy, a Vicar of Christ who governs her visibly. The visibility is, above all, that of the Chair of Peter, on which 266 popes have sat until today.

The pope is a person who occupies a chair, a *cathedra*: there is no cathedra without a person, but the danger exists that the person will lead others to forget the existence of the chair, that is, of the juridical institution that precedes the person.

Papolatry is a false devotion that does not see in the reigning pope one of the 265 successors of Peter, but considers him to be a new Christ on earth, who personalizes, reinterprets, reinvents, and imposes anew the Magisterium of his predecessors, expanding and perfecting the doctrine of Christ. Papolatry, before it is a theological error, is a deformed psychological and moral attitude. Papolatrists are generally conservatives or moderates who deceive themselves on the possibility of reaching good results in life without a fight, without effort. The secret of their life is always to adapt themselves, to bring the best out of every situation. Their watchword is that everything is calm, "there is no need to worry about anything." Reality, for them, never has the character of a drama. The moderates do not want life to be a drama because that would oblige them to assume responsibilities they do not want to assume. But because life is often dramatic, their sense of reality is turned upside down, into an absolute unreality. Faced with the current crisis in the Church, the moderate instinctively denies it. And the most effective way to tranquilize one's own conscience is by affirming that the pope is always right, even when he contradicts himself or his predecessors. At this point, error inevitably passes from the psychological level to the doctrinal one, and it turns into papolatry, the position that the pope must always be obeyed, no matter what he says or does, because the pope is the only and infallible law of the Catholic Faith.

On the doctrinal level, papolatry has its ideological roots in the voluntarism of William of Ockham (1285–1347) who, paradoxically, was a ferocious adversary of the papacy. While Saint Thomas Aquinas affirmed that God, Absolute Truth and Supreme Good, could not will nor do anything contradictory, Ockham held that God could will and do anything, even evil, because evil and good do not exist in themselves, but are made that way by God. For Saint Thomas, something is commanded or forbidden inasmuch as it is ontologically good or evil; for the followers of Ockham, the opposite goes: something is good or bad inasmuch as God has commanded or forbidden it. Once this principle is admitted, not only do morals become relative, but the representative of God on earth, the Vicar of Christ, can then exercise his supreme authority in an absolute and arbitrary manner and the faithful cannot but pay him unconditional obedience.

In reality, obedience to the Church entails for the subject the duty of fulfilling not the will of the superior, but only the will of God. Because of this, obedience is never blind or unconditional. It has its limits in the natural and divine laws, and in the Tradition of the Church, of which the pope is guardian and not creator.

For the papolater, the pope is not the Vicar of Christ on earth, who has the duty of handing on the doctrine he has received, but a successor of Christ who perfects the doctrine of his predecessors, adapting it to changing times. The doctrine of the Gospel is in perpetual evolution, because it coincides with the Magisterium of the reigning pontiff. The "living Magisterium" replaces the perennial Magisterium; it is expressed by pastoral teaching that changes daily, and has its *regula fidei* (rule of faith) in the subject of the authority and not in the object of the transmitted truth.

A consequence of papolatry is the pretext of canonizing all and each of the popes of the past, so that retroactively each words of theirs, every act of governing, is "infallibilized." However, this concerns only the popes following Vatican II and not those who preceded that council.

At this point, there arises a question: The golden era of the history of the Church is the Middle Ages, and yet the only medieval popes canonized by the Church are Leo IX, Gregory VII, and Celestine V. In the twelfth and thirteenth centuries, there were great popes, but none of these were canonized. For seven hundred years, between the fourteenth and twentieth centuries, only Pope Pius V and Pope Pius X were canonized. Were all the others unworthy popes, sinners? Certainly not. But heroism in the governing of the Church is an exception, not the rule, and if all the popes were saints, then nobody is a saint. Sanctity is such an exception that it loses meaning when it becomes the rule. There is a concern that the movement today to canonize all the popes is because we no longer believe in anyone's sanctity. Those who want to learn more about this problem can read to their benefit Christopher Ferrara's article, published in *The Remnant*, dedicated to "The Canonization Crisis."[10]

---

10. See https://remnantnewspaper.com/web/index.php/articles/item/3753-the-canonization-crisis-part-1.

Is a papal diarchy possible?

Papolatry does not exist in an abstract sense: today, for example, we need to speak in a more precise way of Francis-olatry, but also of Benedictolatry, as Miguel Ángel Yáñez observed well on *Adelante la fé*.[11] This papolatry can come to counterpoising pope against pope (as between the followers, for example, of Pope Francis and those of Pope Benedict), or looking for harmony and coexistence between the two popes through imagining a possible division of their roles. What took place on the occasion of the fifth anniversary of the election of Pope Francis in March 2018 was significant and unsettling. All of the media's attention was focused on the case of a letter of Benedict XVI to Pope Francis: a letter that turned out to have been manipulated, and caused the resignation of the head of Vatican communications, Monsignor Dario Viganò. The discussion revealed, however, the existence of a false premise, accepted by all: the existence of a sort of papal diarchy in which there is Pope Francis who carries out its functions, and then another pope, Benedict, who serves the Chair of Peter through prayer and if necessary with counsel. The existence of the two popes is admitted as a done deal: only the nature of their relationship is argued. But the truth is that it is impossible that two popes can exist. The papacy may not be divided up: there can be only one Vicar of Christ.

Benedict XVI had the ability to renounce the papacy, but consequently had also the responsibility to give up the name of Benedict XVI, dressing in white, and the title of pope, emeritus or otherwise: in a word, he would have had to definitively cease from being pope, also leaving Vatican City. Why did he not do so? Because Benedict XVI seems to be convinced of still being pope, although a pope who has

---

11. See https://adelantelafe.com/benedictolatras/.

renounced the exercise of the Petrine ministry. This conviction is born of a profoundly erroneous ecclesiology, founded on a sacramental and not juridical conception of the papacy. If the Petrine *munus* is a sacrament and not a juridical office, then it has an indelible character, but in this case it would be impossible to renounce the office. The resignation presupposes the revocability of the office, and is then irreconcilable with the sacramental vision of the papacy.

Antonio Socci has written a book with the title *Non è Francesco* [He Is Not Francis], in which he proposes that Jorge Mario Bergoglio is not the true pope. It is only a hypothesis. But there is one thing that is certain: "He is not Benedict"—that is to say, Joseph Ratzinger is certainly no longer pope, because he resigned his office, and his resignation is, until the contrary is proven, valid according to Church law.

Cardinal Brandmüller rightly judged the thesis of a *renuntiatio mystica* (mystical resignation) by Benedict XVI, advanced by Professor Valerio Gigliotti,[12] unintelligible, and the attempt to establish a sort of contemporaneous parallelism of a reigning pope and a praying pope impossible. "A two-headed pope would be a monstrosity,"[13] says Cardinal Brandmüller, who adds: "Canon law does not recognize the figure of a Pope Emeritus."[14] "The resignee, consequently, is no longer Bishop of Rome, not even a cardinal."[15]

Regarding the doubts about the election of Pope Francis, the canonical constitutions in force, notes Professor Geraldina Boni,[16] do not sanate [render valid] invalid elections

---

12. Valerio Gigliotti, *La tiara deposta* (Olschki, Firenze 2013), 414.

13. Walter Brandmüller, "Renuntiatio Papae. Alcune riflessioni storico-canonistiche," in *Archivio giuridico* 3–4 (2016), 655–74, at 660.

14. Ibid., 661.

15. Ibid., 660.

16. Geraldina Boni, *Sopra una rinuncia. La decisione di papa Benedetto XVI e il diritto* (Bononia University Press, Bologna 2015).

that are simoniacal or arranged by bargaining, agreements, promises, or other commitments of any other kind among cardinals, like the possible planning of Bergoglio's election described by Austen Ivereigh in the book *The Great Reformer*.[17] Canonists have always taught that peaceful "*universalis ecclesiae adhaesio*" [universal ecclesial acceptance] is a sign and infallible effect of a valid election and legitimate papacy, and the adhesion or acceptance of Pope Francis by the people of God has not yet been doubted by any of the cardinals who participated in the Conclave.

What the professor of the University of Bologna writes matches the observations of others, based on the teachings of the most authoritative theologians and canonists.[18] The acceptance of a pope by the universal Church is an infallible sign of his legitimacy, and heals at the root every defect of the papal election (for example, illegal machinations, conspiracies, etc.). This is also a consequence of the visible character of the Church and of the papacy.

But does Benedict XVI truly represent the antithesis of Pope Francis? Authors such as Enrico Maria Radaelli[19] raise many doubts concerning this proposal.

There are those who say that we need to wait for the next conclave in silence, prayer, and trusting expectation. Years have passed in which we have heard repeated that we need to wait for another Saint Pius X who never comes. Why does he never come? Because the pope is the product of a theological and moral culture, and if the theological and moral culture does not change, from where can the pope come who will

---

17. Austen Ivereigh, *The Great Reformer: Francis and the Making of a Radical Pope* (Henry Holt and Company, New York 2014).

18. See http://www.trueorfalsepope.com/p/is-francis-or-benedict-true-pope.html.

19. Enrico Maria Radaelli, *Al cuore di Ratzinger. Al cuore del mondo* (Edizioni *Pro manuscripto* Aurea Domus, Milano 2018).

resolve the very grave problems the Church is living through today? The popes who have been elected in the past fifty years, even with their differences, have never resolved any problem, because they themselves are sons of unresolved problems; they have become not the solution but the cause of new problems.

If no cardinal has dared to criticize Pope Francis, how can we imagine that a new pope, a product of this College of Cardinals, will be any different from Francis? From where will he produce the courage tomorrow that he does not have today?

A nemine est judicandus, nisi a fide devius

The juridical character of the Petrine office is described well by a canonist above all suspicion, the former rector of the Gregorian University, Jesuit Father Gianfranco Ghirlanda, who during the time of transition between the last two pontificates dedicated a clear article in *La Civiltà Cattolica* to "The Vacancy of the Roman See." "The vacancy of the Roman See occurs in case of the cessation of the office on the part of the Roman Pontiff, which happens for four reasons: 1) Death; 2) Sure and perpetual insanity or complete mental infirmity; 3) Notorious apostasy, heresy, schism; 4) Resignation."

Father Ghirlanda explains:

In the first case, the Apostolic See is vacant from the moment of death of the Roman Pontiff; in the second and in the third from the moment of the declaration on the part of the cardinals; in the fourth from the moment of the renunciation. The criterion, then, is the safeguard of ecclesial communion itself. There, where this no longer exists on the part of the pope, he cannot have any more power, because, *ipso iure* (by the law itself), he would fall from his primatial office.

At this point, Father Ghirlanda lingers on the case of a heretical pope. There is no reference to a specific pope, since

in February 2013 no one had yet been elected. Father Ghirlanda refers to an "academic example":

> There is the case, admitted by doctrine, of notorious apos-
> tasy, heresy, and schism, into which the Roman Pontiff
> could fall, but as a "private doctor," that does not demand
> the assent of the faithful, because by faith in the personal
> infallibility that the Roman Pontiff has in the carrying out
> of his office, and therefore in the assistance of the Holy
> Ghost, we must say that he cannot make heretical affirma-
> tions, wishing to utilize his primatial authority, because if
> he were to do so, he would fall *ipso iure* from his office.
> However, in such cases, because "the first see is judged by
> no one" [canon 1404] no one could depose the Roman
> Pontiff, but only a declaration of the fact could be made,
> which would have to be [done] on the part of the Cardi-
> nals, at least of those present in Rome. Such an eventuality,
> however, although foreseen in doctrine, is held to be
> totally unlikely, by the intervention of Divine Providence
> in favor of the Church.[20]

Father Ghirlanda is, in this exposition, neither a traditional-
ist nor a progressivist but a scholar who has gathered together a thousand years of canonical tradition.

If in the field of philosophy and theology the undisputed
summit of Christian thought is represented by Saint Thomas
Aquinas, in the field of canon law the equivalent of that school
is represented by Gratian (Magister Gratianus) and his disciples. Recalling an assertion of Saint Boniface, bishop of
Mainz, cited by Ivo of Chartres, Gratian affirmed that the
pope "*a nemine est iudicandus, nisi deprehendatur a fide
devius*" [is judged by no one, except when he is caught having
deviated from the Faith].[21] This principle is reiterated in the

20. Gianfranco Ghirlanda, "Cessazione dall'ufficio di Romano Ponte-
fice," *La Civiltà Cattolica*, n. 3905 (March 2, 2013), 445–62, at 445.
21. Gratianus, *Decretum,* Pars I, Dist. XL.

Summa decretorum by Huguccio, or Hugh of Pisa,[22] considered the most famous *magister decretorum*, master of decrees, of the twelfth century.

The possibility of judging the pope if he renders himself guilty of heresy, as attested by Monsignor Victor Martin, an authoritative historian of the Church, was "for all of the Middle Ages an uncontested maxim."[23] Father Salvatore Vacca, who traced the history of the axiom *prima sedes a nemine judicatur* [the First See is judged by no one], recalled that "the thesis of the possibility of a heretical pope would be held in consideration ... during the whole of the Middle Ages, until the time of the Western Schism (1379–1417)."[24]

In the case of a heretical pope, the principle according to which *prima sedes a nemine judicatur* is not violated, in the first place because, according to canonical tradition, this principle admits only one exception, the case of heresy; in the second place because the cardinals would be limited to merely certifying the fact of heresy, as if they were certifying the loss of mental faculties, without exercising any deposition of the Roman Pontiff. The cessation of the primatial office would only be acknowledged and declared by them.

Theologians argue whether the loss of the pontificate would arrive at the moment in which the pope falls into heresy or only in the case of the heresy becoming manifest or notorious, and publicly spread.

Arnaldo Xavier da Silveira[25] holds that although an incompatibility *in radice* (at the root) exists between heresy

22. Huguccio Pisanus, *Summa Decretorum*, Part I, Dist. XL, ch. 6.

23. Victor Martin, "Comment s'est formée la doctrine de la supériorité du Concile sur le Pape," in *Revue des Sciences Religieuses* 2 (1937), 127.

24. Salvatore Vacca, "Prima Sedes a nemine judicatur," in *Genesi e sviluppo storico dell'assioma fino al Decreto di Graziano* (Pontificia Università Gregoriana, Rome 1993), 254.

25. Arnaldo Xavier da Silveira, *Ipotesi teologica di un Papa eretico* (Solfanelli, Chieti 2016).

and papal jurisdiction, the pope does not lose his office until the time when his heresy becomes manifest. The Church being a visible and perfect society, the loss of the faith by her visible Head would need to be a public fact. As a tree can live for a certain time after its roots have been severed, so can jurisdiction be maintained precariously by the possessor, even after a fall into heresy. Jesus Christ maintains the person of the heretical pontiff in his jurisdiction provisionally, until the Church recognizes the deposition.

Cardinal Journet, following Cardinal Cajetan and John of Saint Thomas, holds that even after a manifest sin of heresy, the pope would not be deposed until after one or two public admonitions as Saint Paul foresees (Tit 3:10). Only by persisting in heresy after a repeated admonition would the pope lose the papacy.

> The action of the Church is simply declarative; she manifests that there is an incorrigible sin of heresy: then the authoritative action of God is exerted to sever the papacy from a subject who, persisting in heresy after admonition, becomes, according to Divine Law, unfit to hold the office any longer. So by virtue of the Scripture, the Church designates and God deposes.[26]

What is certain is that recognizing the possibility of a pope falling into heresy does not mean in any way diminishing love for and devotion to the papacy. It means admitting that the pope is the vicar, not always impeccable and not always infallible, of Jesus Christ, who is the only Head of the Mystical Body of the Church.

Against catacombism

The theme of the visibility of the Church is an argument to

---

26. Charles Journet, *L'Eglise du Verbe incarné. Essai de Théologie spéculative*, vol. II: *Sa structure interne et son unité catholique* (Desclée de Brouwer, Paris 1955), 266.

combat another temptation widespread today: that of cata-combism. Catacombism is the attitude of those who retreat from the battlefield and hide themselves in the illusion of being able to survive without fighting. Catacombism is the denial of the militant conception of Christianity.

The catacombist does not wish to fight, because he is convinced of having already lost the battle; he accepts the situation of the inferiority of Catholics in the culture as a given, without going back to the causes that have determined it. But if Catholics today are in the minority, it is because they have lost a series of battles; they have lost these battles because they have not fought them; they have not fought them because they have removed the very idea of the "enemy," turning their backs on the Augustinian concept of the two cities fighting each other in history, the only concept that can offer us an explanation of what is happening, and what has happened. If one rejects this militant concept, one accepts the principle of the irreversibility of the historic process, and from catacombism one inevitably passes to progressivism and modernism. The catacombists oppose the Constantinian Church to the Minority and Persecuted Church of the first three centuries. But Pius XII in his address to Catholic Action on December 8, 1947 refutes this theory, explaining that the Catholics of the first three centuries were not cata-combists, but conquerors.

Not rarely has the Church of the first centuries been represented as "the Church of the catacombs," as if the Christians of that time were used to living there, hidden. There is nothing more inaccurate: those subterranean necropolises, destined principally for the burial of the faithful departed, did not serve as places of refuge, except perhaps sometimes during violent persecutions. The life of Christians, in those centuries marked by blood, was carried out in the midst of the streets and houses, in the open. These "did not live secluded from the world; they frequented, as others, the forum, the baths, the workshops, the shops, the markets, the public squares; they exercised their professions as sailors, soldiers, farmers and merchants."[27] Wishing to portray that valorous Church, always ready to live on the forefront, as a community of draft dodgers, hiding themselves for embarrassment or cowardice, would be an insult to their virtues. They were fully aware of their duty of conquering the world for Christ, to transform private and public life according to the doctrine and law of the Divine Savior, out of which a new civilization could be born—another Rome, springing forth from the tombs of the two Princes of the Apostles. And they reached their goal. Rome and the Roman Empire became Christian.

In times past it was said that the Sacrament of Confirmation made us "soldiers of Christ," and Pius XII, addressing the bishops of the United States, said: "The Christian, if he does honor to the name he bears, is always an apostle; it is not permitted to the Soldier of Christ that he quit the battlefield, because only death puts an end to his military service."[28] We need to recover this militant conception of the Christian life.

The strength of silence and the strength of speech

There are those who say that we need to give up action and the fight, because by now there is nothing left to do on a human level. We need to wait for an extraordinary intervention of Divine Providence. Many waited for this miraculous event in 2017, the centenary year of Fatima, but nothing happened. Why? Maybe the reason is that the wait for this miraculous intervention was, for them, the pretext for justifying the renunciation of action. Certainly it is God, and He alone, who guides and changes history. But God requires the

27. Tertullian, *Apologeticum*, c. 42.
28. Pius XII, Discourse to the Bishops of the United States, November 1, 1939.

cooperation of men, and if men cease working, divine grace will also cease to act. In fact, as Saint Ambrose observed, "the divine benefits are not passed to him who sleeps, but to him who watches."[29]

There are those who say that we need to forego not only action, but even speech. Sometimes we meet someone who, with his finger at his lips, and eyes raised to Heaven, tells us that we need to keep quiet and pray, nothing else. But it would be an error to make silence a rule of behavior, because on the day of judgment, we will answer not only for vain words, but also for guilty silences.

There are vocations to silence, like those of many contemplative monks and nuns; but Catholics, from pastors to the last of the faithful, have the duty of testifying to their Faith, with words and example. It was through the Word that the Apostles won over the world and the Gospel was spread from one end of the earth to the other.

Saint Athanasius and Saint Hilary did not remain silent against the Arians, nor did Saint Peter Damian against the corrupt prelates of his time. Saint Catherine of Siena did not keep silent in front of the popes of her time, nor did Saint Vincent Ferrer presenting himself as the Angel of the Apocalypse. In recent times, these did not keep quiet but spoke: the bishop of Münster, Clemens August von Galen, in the face of Nazism; and Cardinal József Mindszenty, primate of Hungary, confronted by Communism.

Today, moreover, silence is not used as a moment of recollection and of reflection that prepares one for battle, but as a political strategy, an alternative to fighting—a silence that predisposes us for dissimulation, hypocrisy, and final surrender. Day after day, month after month, year after year, the politics of silence has become a jail that imprisons many conservatives. In this sense, silence is not only a sin of today, but

29. St. Ambrose, *Expos. Evang. sec. Luc.*, IV, 49.

is also a chastisement for yesterday's sins. Today, those who for too many years remained silent are prisoners of silence. However, he is free who in the course of the last fifty years has not kept silent, but has spoken openly and without compromises, because only the Truth makes us free (Jn 8:32).

"*Tempus est tacendi, tempus loquendi*," says Ecclesiastes 3:7. "There is a time to keep silence, and a time to speak." And today is the moment to speak.

To speak means, above all, to witness publicly to one's own fidelity to the Gospel and to immutable Catholic truths, denouncing the errors that counteract it. In times of crisis, the rule is that which Benedict XV in the encyclical *Ad Beatissimi Apostolorum* of November 1, 1914 declared against the modernists: "It is Our will that the law of our forefathers should still be held sacred: 'Let there be no innovation; keep to what has been handed down': *nihil innovetur nisi quod traditum est*."[30] Sacred Tradition remains the criterion for discerning that which is Catholic and that which is not, rendering resplendent the visible marks of the Church. Tradition is the faith of the Church that the popes have maintained and transmitted throughout the course of the centuries. But Tradition comes before the pope and not the pope before Tradition.

Limiting ourselves, then, to a generic denunciation of the errors that oppose the Tradition of the Church isn't enough. It is for us to call out by name all those who inside the Church profess a theology, a philosophy, a morality, a spirituality in contrast with the perennial Magisterium of the Church, no matter what office they may occupy. And today we must admit that the pope himself promotes and propagates errors and heresies in the Church. We need to have the courage to say this, with all the veneration that is due to the

---

30. Pope St. Stephen I, *Letter to Saint Cyprian*, in Denzinger, n. 110, 4.

pope. True devotion to the papacy expresses itself in an attitude of filial resistance, as happened in the *Filial Correction* addressed to Pope Francis in 2017.

But there isn't only a *tempus loquendi*, a time to speak. There is also a *modus loquendi*, a way to speak—a way the Catholic should express himself. The correction has to be filial, as it was: respectful, devout, without sarcasm, without irreverence, without contempt, without bitter zeal, without gratification, without pride, with a profound spirit of charity, which is love for God and love for the Church.

In the crisis of our day, it seems that every profession of faith and declaration of fidelity that has been issued lacks strength, clarity, and sincerity, because they have disregarded the responsibility of Pope Francis for the crisis. We need to have the courage to say: Holy Father, you are the first one responsible for the confusion that exists today in the Church; Holy Father, you are the first one responsible for the heresies circulating in the Church today. The first one, but not the only one who is responsible. The responsibility has to be extended to him who adorns himself with the title of Pope Emeritus, to him who claims continuity between this pontificate and the preceding one, to him who is the cause of this pontificate: Benedict XVI.

The responsibility, finally, cannot fail to involve the cardinals who are silent, and who, remaining silent, fail to perform their duty as counselors and collaborators of the pope.

Yet it is not enough to denounce the pastors who demolish—or favor the demolition of—the Church. We must reduce to the indispensable minimum our ecclesiastical cohabitation with them, as happens in an agreement of matrimonial separation. If a father exercises physical or moral violence toward his wife and children, the wife, although recognizing the validity of the marriage itself, and without requesting an annulment, can request a separation to protect herself and her children. The Church permits it. In our case, giving up living habitually together means distancing oneself from the teachings and practices of the evil pastors, refusing to participate in the programs and activities promoted by them.

But we must not forget that the Church cannot disappear. Therefore, it is necessary to support the apostolate of shepherds who remain faithful to the traditional teachings of the Church, participating in their initiatives and encouraging them to speak, to act, and to guide the disoriented flock.

It is time to separate ourselves from evil pastors, and to unite ourselves to the good ones, inside of the one Church in which both the wheat and the cockle live in the same field (Mt 13:24–30), remembering that the Church is visible, and cannot save herself apart from her legitimate pastors.

The Church is visible and will save herself with the pope, not without the pope. We need to renew the bond of love and veneration that joins us to the successor of Peter, above all with prayer, so Jesus Christ will give him and all prelates the necessary strength not to betray the sacred deposit of the Faith, and, if this were to take place, to restore true guidance to the abandoned sheepfold. Only one supreme and solemn voice can bring an end to the process of self-destruction now in play: that of the Roman Pontiff, the only voice to which was guaranteed the possibility of defining the Word of Christ, making itself the infallible mouthpiece of Tradition.

The infallibility of the Magisterium of the pope, together with the universal primacy of governing, constitutes the foundation on which Jesus Christ instituted His Church, and on which she will remain firm, thanks to the divine promise, until the end of time. But the pope must *teach*, fulfilling the conditions of the First Vatican Council, in a solemn and definitive manner, obligating the faithful to believe that which he clarifies and defines in the vast field of faith and morals.

It is necessary that the Supreme Pontiff exercise in all power and breadth, not only the power of the Magisterium, but also the power of governance, which he derives from his primacy of jurisdiction. The ecclesiastical *potestas* (power) has to be exercised through the application of penal sanctions against all those who put revealed Truth up for discussion. Only the pope can do this, and we renew our request to the Vicar of Christ.

And yet, even if the Vicar of Christ would betray his mission, the Holy Spirit would never cease to assist, not even for a moment, His Church, in which even in times of defection from the Faith a remnant, even a small one, of pastors and faithful will continue to always keep and pass on Tradition, trusting in the divine promise: "I am with you all days, even to the consummation of the world" (Mt 28:20).

In his encyclical *Fulgens Radiatur* of March 21, 1947, for the fourteenth centenary of the death of Saint Benedict, Pius XII said:

> Whoever considers his [Saint Benedict's] celebrated life and studies, in the light of the truth of history, the gloomy and stormy times in which he lived, will without doubt realize the truth of the divine promise Christ made to the Apostles and to the society He founded: "I am with you all days, even to the consummation of the world" [Mt 28:20]. At no time in history does this promise lose its force; it is verified in the course of all ages flowing, as they do, under the guidance of Divine Providence. But when enemies assail the Christian name more fiercely, when the fateful barque of Peter is tossed about more violently, and when everything seems to be tottering with no hope of human support, it is then that Christ is present, Bondsman, Comforter, Source of supernatural power, and raises up fresh champions to protect Catholicism, to restore it to its former vigor, and give it even greater increase under the inspiration and help of heavenly grace.

For those who remain faithful to Tradition in times of crisis, their model is the Most Blessed Virgin Mary, who alone kept the Faith on Holy Saturday, and who, after the Ascension of Our Lord into Heaven, did not keep silent but sustained with all the firmness and clearness of her words the nascent Church. Her Heart was, and remains, the Treasure Chest of the Church.[31]

Those truly devoted to Mary, about whom Saint Louis-Marie Grignion de Montfort speaks, are also the true devotees of the papacy, who in times of defection by the authorities and the obscuring of the Faith will not hesitate to brandish "the two-edged sword of the Word of God" (Heb 4:12), with which "they will pierce through and through, for life and for death, those against whom they are sent by Almighty God."[32]

Their battle against the enemies of God will bring closer the triumph of the Immaculate Heart of Mary, which will also be the triumph of the papacy and of the restored Church.

31. St. Bonaventure, *De Nativitate B. Virginis Mariae Sermo V*, in *Opera* IX, 717.
32. St. Louis Marie Grignion de Montfort, *True Devotion to Mary*, n. 57.

1517, 1717, 1917:
Three Revolutions and
Fatima[1]

A S IN THE LIVES of men, anniversaries are also celebrated in the lives of peoples, and 2017 is full of anniversaries; not all anniversaries, however, merit a cake
with candles.

The most talked-about anniversary has been Martin
Luther's. Five hundred years have passed since October 31,
1517, when Luther nailed his 95 theses on the great door of
the Wittenberg Cathedral, an action that would set in
motion the so-called Protestant Reformation and mark the
end of medieval Christendom.

Two centuries later, on June 29, 1717, the Grand Lodge of
London was founded. This event is considered the birth of
modern Freemasonry, which in turn is directly connected to
the French Revolution. The Masonic Lodges were in effect
the intellectual laboratories in which the Revolution of 1789
was hatched.

On October 26 or November 7, 1917, depending on
whether the Gregorian or the Julian calendar is adopted,
Lenin and Trotsky's Bolshevik Party occupied the Winter
Palace in St. Petersburg. Thus, the Russian Revolution
entered history and has yet to leave it.

1517, 1717, and 1917, then, are three symbolic dates, three

---

1. A lecture given at the Cosmos Club in Washington, D.C., March 27,
2017.

events that are part of a single process. Pius XII, in his speech to the men of Catholic Action on October 12, 1952, summed it up like this: "Christ yes, Church no" (the Protestant revolution against the Church); "then: God yes, Christ no" (the Masonic revolution against the central mysteries of Christianity); "finally, the impious cry: God is dead; indeed: God never was" (the atheistic Communist revolution). "And here is the attempt to build the structure of the world upon foundations that We do not hesitate to point out as the principles responsible for the danger that threatens mankind." Three stages of a single process, now reaching its pinnacle: the Church called it Revolution, with a capital *R*, to describe its metaphysical essence and historical, centuries-old significance.

Yet there is a fourth anniversary that, till now, has been discussed very little. 2017 is also the first centenary of the Fatima apparitions, and it is in light of the Fatima message that I propose to examine the three revolutions that are commemorated this year.

Some principles to remember

The first element to emphasize is that we are speaking here about historical facts.

The apparitions of Our Lady at Fatima between May 13 and October 13, 1917 are an objective historical fact, not a subjective religious experience of Our Lady appearing to the three little shepherds.

Historians imbued by rationalism, including many Catholic ones, would like to expel all that is supernatural from history—miracles, revelations, and heavenly messages—consigning them to the "private sphere" of faith. However, these miracles, these apparitions, and these messages, when they are authentic, are part of history, in the same way as war and peace and all that happens in history and which history records.

1517, 1717, 1917: Three Revolutions and Fatima

The Fatima apparitions were events that happened in a precise place at a particular moment in history—events verified by thousands of witnesses and a thorough canonical investigation, which ended in 1930. Six popes in the twentieth century publicly acknowledged the Fatima apparitions, even if none of them fully complied with Our Lady's requests. Paul VI, John Paul II, and Benedict XVI visited the sanctuary as popes, while John XXIII and John Paul I went there when they were still Cardinals Roncalli and Luciani. Pius XII sent his delegate, Cardinal Aloisi Masella. All of them honored Fatima.

But the message of Fatima represents a historical event for another reason: it is a private revelation not only for the spiritual good of those who received it—the three little shepherds—but for all of humanity.

The Church makes a distinction between public Revelation and private revelations. The public Revelation of the Church ended with the death of the last Evangelist, St. John. However, St. Thomas Aquinas teaches that revelations and heavenly prophecies continue even after the conclusion of public Revelation, not to complete or propose new doctrine, but to direct the behavior of men in conforming to it.[2] Sometimes private revelations are directly solely toward the spiritual perfection of those who receive these supernatural gifts. At other times, as in the case of the Sacred Heart messages to St. Margaret Mary Alacoque, they are directed to the good of the Church and all of society. The Sacred Heart of Jesus is at the center of the Paray-le-Monial revelations and the Immaculate Heart of Mary is at the center of those from Fatima. Fatima and Paray-le-Monial are private revelations for all of mankind. They have the characteristics of great "spiritual direction" that the Lord offers us to guide the behavior of men at certain times in history.

2. St. Thomas Aquinas, *Summa Theologiae*, II-II, q. 174, a. 6, ad 3.

A third principle arises from the fact that some private revelations, like Fatima, are reserved not for the good of single individuals but for the whole of society in a determinate historical period. Private revelations help us to interpret the historical times we live in, but the times we live in help us in turn to understand more deeply the significance of the revelations. Thus there is a reciprocality. If it is true that divine words project light in the darkest ages of history, the opposite is also true: the course of historical events helps us to understand the meaning, at times obscure, of prophecies and revelations. In the centenary of the Fatima apparitions, it is necessary then to read Our Lady's words in light of what happened during the last century, a ravaged century,[3] to make sure that the light of this message illuminates with greater clarity the darkness of the times we are now living in.

The Russian Revolution of 1917

The historical background against which the Fatima apparitions took place is that of a terrible war, historically called "The Great War": the war between 1914 and 1918 that saw more than nine million victims in Europe alone. A holocaust of blood, defined in that very year 1917 by Pope Benedict XV as a "useless massacre."[4] It was a massacre useful only to the anti-Christian Revolution that saw in the war the chance "to republicanize Europe"[5] and to complete the goals of the French Revolution.

The war overturned the political order that had been in force in Europe since 1815: that of the Congress of Vienna, which saw a Holy Alliance between the Empires of Austria

---

3. Robert Conquest, *Reflections on a Ravaged Century* (W. W. Norton & Company, New York 2001).

4. Benedict XV, Letter of August 1, 1917, in AAS IX (1917), 421–23.

5. Ferenc Fejtő, *Requiem pour un empire défunt* (Lieu Commun, Paris 1988), 308, 311.

and Russia against the liberal Revolution. The troops of the Hapsburg Empire and those of the Germans, lined up on the eastern front, contributed to the collapse of the Czarist Empire.

On April 3, 1917, a month before the apparitions, the head of the Bolshevik sect, Vladimir Ilyich Lenin (1870–1924), until then in exile in Zurich,[6] returned to Russia in a sealed train car made available by the German Joint Chief of Staff, who wanted to make Russia fall into complete chaos. Lenin set fire to Russia. However, the end never justifies the means, and the chaos swept through not only Russia, but the entire world.

The same year, on January 13, 1917, Leon Trotsky—another Russian revolutionary—and his family crossed the Atlantic Ocean and landed in New York. Antony Sutton posed a good question: "How did Trotsky, who knew only German and Russian, survive in capitalist America?"[7] What is certain is that American President Woodrow Wilson provided Trotsky with a passport to return to Russia to "carry forward" the Revolution.[8] In August an American Red Cross mission, made up of lawyers and financiers, arrived in Petrograd. The mission was in fact a mission of Wall Street financiers to influence and pave the way for control, through either Alexander Kerensky (1881–1970) or the Bolshevik revolutionaries, of the Russian markets and resources.[9]

There was then a convergence of interests among the German military and American financiers. This cloaks the origins of the Russian Revolution in a certain mystery.

The Russian Revolution started by Lenin was carried out

6. Alexander Solzhenitsyn, *Lenin in Zurich* (Book Club Associates, London 1976).

7. Anthony Sutton, *Wall Street and the Bolshevik Revolution* (Arlington House, New Rochelle 1974), 22.

8. Ibid., 25.

9. Ibid., 86–88.

in two stages: the first was the so-called February Revolution, which led to the abdication of the Czar and the installation of a liberal-democratic republic, under the leadership of Kerensky. The second stage was the October Revolution, which brought about the fall of Kerensky and the installation of Lenin and Trotsky's Communist regime. There then opened up a killing season of no historical precedent.

The Russian Revolution, like the French Revolution, was the work of a minority, and was carried out with surprising rapidity, without anyone being quite aware of what was happening. John Reed, an American journalist and socialist who took part in the Revolution, wrote a book entitled *Ten Days that Shook the World*, in which he vividly describes the atmosphere of those days:

> Superficially all was quiet; hundreds of thousands of people retired at a prudent hour, got up early, and went to work. In Petrograd the streetcars were running, the stores and restaurants open, theaters going, an exhibition of paintings advertised.... All the complex routine of common life—humdrum even in wartime—proceeded as usual. Nothing is so astounding as the vitality of the social organism—how it persists, feeding itself, clothing itself, amusing itself, in the face of the worst calamities.[10]

Fatima 1917

The Russian Revolution was not only a historical event, it was a philosophical event. In his *Theses on Feuerbach* (1845), Karl Marx argues that the task of the philosopher is not that of interpreting the world, but of transforming it.[11] The revo-

10. John Reed, *Ten Days that Shook the World* (Boni and Liveright, New York 1919), 112.

11. *Theses on Feuerbach*, Italian translation in Feuerbach, Marx, Engels, *Materialismo dialettico e materialismo storico*, ed. Cornelio Fabro (La Scuola, Brescia 1962), 81–86.

lutionary has to demonstrate in praxis the potency and efficacy of his thought. In achieving power, Lenin performed a philosophical act; he didn't theorize the Revolution, but brought it about. In a manner of speaking, Marx and Engels's socialism, thanks to Lenin, became "incarnate" in history. The Russian Revolution appears then as a diabolical parody of the mystery of the Incarnation. Jesus, by becoming incarnate, wanted to open up the gates of Heaven to men: the Marxist Revolution closed the gates of Heaven in order to make of the Earth its impossible paradise. It was an irruption of the demonic into history.

However, Heaven responded with an irruption of the sacred upon the earth. At the other end of Europe, during those same months, something else was taking place.

On May 13, 1917, at the Cova de Iria—an isolated place of rocks and olive trees near the village of Fatima in Portugal— "a lady dressed all in white, more brilliant than the sun, shedding rays of light, clearer and stronger than a crystal glass filled with the most sparkling water, pierced by the burning rays of the sun," appeared to three children who were watching over their sheep: Francesco and Jacinta Marto and their little cousin Lucia dos Santos. This Lady revealed herself as the Mother of God, entrusted with a message for mankind as she had been before in Paris (at the Rue du Bac) in 1838 and at Lourdes in 1858. Our Lady gave an appointment to the three shepherd-children for the thirteenth of every subsequent month until October. There were six apparitions. The last apparition ended with a great miracle, a wondrous seal from Heaven: "the dance of the sun," witnessed by thousands of people who were able to describe it in great detail and which was seen even from 25 miles away.[12]

12. Martins dos Reis, *O Milagre do Sol e o Segredo de Fátima* (Ed. Salesianas, Porto 1966).

From that moment on, the histories of Fatima and of Russia have been intertwined.

The history of the twentieth century, and that of the twenty-first until now, has seen the struggle between the children of light and the children of darkness. The first nourish themselves on what we might call the spirit of Fatima; the second on the spirit of the Prince of Darkness, which in the twentieth century was manifested above all under the form of Communism and its metamorphoses.

The Secret of Fatima

Even more than a place, Fatima is a message.

The message revealed by Our Lady at Fatima contains three parts, called secrets, which form an organic, coherent whole. The first is a terrifying vision of hell into which the souls of sinners precipitate; the mercy of the Immaculate Heart of Mary counters this punishment and is the supreme remedy offered by God to humanity for the salvation of souls.

The second part involves a dramatic historical alternative: peace—the fruit of the conversion of the world and the fulfillment of Our Lady's requests—or else a terrible chastisement that would await mankind if it remained obstinate in its sinful ways. Russia would be the instrument of this chastisement.

The third part, divulged by the Holy See in June 2000, expands on the tragedy in the life of the Church, offering a vision of a pope and bishops, religious and laity struck dead by persecutors. Discussions that have opened up in recent years about this "Third Secret" risk, however, obscuring the prophetic force of the message's central part, summed up in two decisive sentences: Russia "will scatter her errors throughout the world"; and "in the end, my Immaculate Heart will triumph."

1517, 1717, 1917: Three Revolutions and Fatima

"Russia will scatter her errors throughout the world." The term "errors" is precise: error is the denial of the truth. Truth, then, exists, and there is only one truth: that which is preserved and diffused by the Catholic Church. Russia's errors are those of an ideology that opposes the natural and Christian order by denying God, religion, the family, and private property. This complex of errors has a name—Communism—and has in Russia its universal center of diffusion.

Too often Communism has been identified with a purely political regime, neglecting its ideological dimension, whereas it is precisely its doctrinal dimension that Our Lady highlights.

The anti-Communist movement of the twentieth century often seemed to identify only the Communism of the Soviet tanks or the Gulags, which are certainly an expression of Communism, but not its heart. Pius XI emphasized the ideologically perverse nature of Communism. "For the first time in history," he stated in his encyclical *Divini Redemptoris* of March 19, 1937, "we are witnessing a struggle, cold-blooded in purpose and mapped out to the least detail, between man and 'all that is called God' (2 Thess 1:4)."

Many anti-Communists have neglected this aspect, under the illusion of arriving at a possible compromise with a "humanitarian" Communism, purified of any violence. They have not understood the intrinsic ideological malice in Communism. What are the origins of this ideological malice? The Communists themselves sum up their errors in the formula of dialectic materialism: the universe is matter in evolution and Hegelian dialectic is the soul of this evolution. This philosophical, pantheistic vision has its political expression in a classless society. Social and political egalitarianism derives from metaphysical egalitarianism, which not only denies the distinction between God and man, but by divinizing matter denies every distinction between men and created things.

The genealogy of errors

Errors do not spring up from nowhere. Russia's errors, like all errors, sprang forth from previous errors and they, in turn, generate further errors. In order to fully understand their nature, we need to ask where these errors came from and where they are taking us.

Communism's base text is *The Manifesto of the Communist Party*, published by Karl Marx (1818–1883) and Friedrich Engels (1820–1895) in February 1848. This text was commissioned from Marx and Engels by The League of the Just, a Communist group devoted to the ultra-Jacobin ideas of Gracchus Babeuf (1760–1797). Among the direct precursors of Socialism, Engels counts alongside the Jacobins the Anabaptists, the "levelers" of the English Revolution, and the philosophers of the Enlightenment in the eighteenth century.[13]

The Anabaptists represent the far left of the Protestant Revolution, what the historian George Huntston Williams (1914–2000) described as the radical Reformation, as opposed to the supposedly moderate Reformation of Luther and Calvin.[14] But in reality, these two movements were not opposed at all: the Anabaptists were simply a development of what Luther had started. What characterizes all Revolutions is that their potentialities are contained in their ideological origin. The principles at the roots of Anabaptism originate from the impetus that Luther from the very beginning had given to the religious revolution of the sixteenth century.

Professor Plinio Corrêa de Oliveira observed:

> Like cataclysms, evil passions have an immense power—but only to destroy. In the first instant of its great explo-

13. Frederick Engels, *The Development of Socialism. From Utopia to Science* (1878), Italian translation (Editori Riuniti, Rome 1958), 15–17.

14. George H. Williams, *The Radical Reformation* (Westminster Press, Philadelphia 1962).

sions, this power already has the potential for all the viru-
lence it will manifest in its worst excesses. In the first
denials of Protestantism, for example, the anarchic yearn-
ings of communism were already implicit. While Luther
was, from the viewpoint of his explicit formulations, no
more than Luther, all the tendencies, states of soul, and
imponderables of the Lutheran explosion already bore
within them, authentically and fully, even though implicitly, the spirit of Voltaire and Robespierre and of Marx and
Lenin.[15]

We need to emphasize a second point here. It is true that
"ideas have consequences,"[16] but not all consequences are
coherent with the intentions. A German philosopher, Wil-
helm Wundt (1832–1920), coined the expression "heterogony
of ends [*Heterogonie der Zwecke*]" to describe the contradictions that often exist between the intentions of man and the
consequences of his actions. This heterogony of ends is typical of all utopias, which in denying reality are doomed to be
contradicted by it.

Luther, for example, emphasized faith alone, denying any
value to human reason. Yet at the same time he denied the
Church's authority in the name of *sola Scriptura*, interpreted
according to the principle of free examination. The Italian
Anabaptists, known as Socinians because they follow the
ideas of the Sienese heretics Lelio (1525–1562) and Fausto
Socino (1539–1604), ascribe a primary role to reason, thus
demolishing the very texts of Holy Scripture with their criti-
cism.

Socinianism is a form of radical Protestantism that moved
from Italy to Poland, where it flourished between the sixteenth and seventeenth centuries; it then migrated to Holland, and from Holland it reached England at the time of the

15. Plinio Correa de Oliveira, *Revolution and Counter-Revolution*, 25.
16. Richard M. Weaver, *Ideas Have Consequences* (The University of
Chicago Press, Chicago and London 2013 [1948]).

English Revolution. Socinianism is a point of passage between religious sects of the Anabaptist types in the seventeenth and eighteenth centuries and the philosophical sects of a Masonic structure in the eighteenth century. In the "lay temple" of social virtues—the Masonic Lodge—the cult of a new ethic freed from the bonds of all dogma and religious morality was practiced.

The relationships between Socinianism and Freemasonry can be followed through the figure of John Toland (1670–1722), author of a work entitled *Pantheisticon* (1720), in which he illustrates the doctrine and the organization of a society of "*sodales socratici* [socratic associations]," which were presented as centers not only for philosophical and political discussion but also for an esoteric introduction to pantheism, and proposed to their members the realization of an egalitarian republic, free of every form of "religious superstition."[17] Pantheism and egalitarianism are always connected.

In 1723, after the foundation of the Grand Lodge, Presbyterian clergyman James Anderson published *The Constitutions of the Free-Masons*. This work was reprinted in Philadelphia in 1734 by Benjamin Franklin (1706–1790), who was that year elected Grand Master of Masons in Pennsylvania. In December 1776, Franklin was dispatched to France by the Continental Congress as ambassador of the United States to the court of Louis XVI. During his stay in France, Benjamin Franklin was active as a Freemason, serving as Venerable Master of the Lodge *Les Neufs Soeurs*. The foundation of the Grand Orient in 1773 marked the beginning of a new phase: a political campaign outside the lodges. Freemasons controlled the elections of March/April 1789 in France and a bloc was formed in the third estate that was led by Masonry. Among the associates of the French lodge was

17. Margaret C. Jacob, *The Newtonians and the English Revolution* (Cornell University Press, Ithaca 1976).

1517, 1717, 1917: Three Revolutions and Fatima

Count Mirabeau (1749–1791), the former French ambassador in Berlin and an orator and statesman, who in early 1791 would be elected president of the National Assembly.

The late Librarian of Congress and historian James H. Billington writes:

> Mirabeau pioneered in applying the evocative language of traditional religion to the new political institutions of revolutionary France. As early as May 10, 1789, he wrote to the constituents who had elected him to the Third Estate that the purpose of the Estates-General was not to reform but "to regenerate" the nation. He subsequently called the National Assembly "the inviolable priesthood of national policy," the Declaration of the Rights of Man "a political gospel," and the Constitution of 1791 a new religion "for which the people are ready to die."[18]

Mirabeau was a member of the Illuminati of Bavaria, a secret society founded in 1776 by Adam Weishaupt, a professor of canon law at Ingolstadt University in Germany. The two prime source books for our knowledge of Adam Weishaupt's Illuminati conspiracy are Professor John Robison's *Proofs of a Conspiracy*, first published in 1798, and the Abbé Augustin Barruel's four-volume study, *Memoirs Illustrating the History of Jacobinism*, published in 1799. I recommend getting acquainted with these books. The purpose of the Order was to destroy all religions, overthrow all governments, and abolish private property.

The Russian Revolution did not arise spontaneously, but was the outcome of a process with deep historical roots. The Communist theorist Antonio Gramsci (1891–1937) sums up this revolutionary process in the formula "philosophy of praxis": "The philosophy of praxis is the crowning point of this entire movement; . . . it corresponds to the nexus of the

---

18. James H. Billington, *Fire in the Minds of Men: Origins of the Revolutionary Faith* (Basic Books, New York 1980), 19–20.

Protestant Reformation plus the French Revolution. It is a philosophy that is also a politics, and a politics that is also a philosophy."[19]

The Revolution betrayed

However, a false philosophy, when it is politicized—that is, when it is carried out in praxis—always betrays its premises. Only the truth is coherent with itself. Error is always contradictory. In this sense, the Revolution can only establish itself if it betrays itself. Like every revolution, the Communist October Revolution was a revolution betrayed. The debate between Stalin and Trotsky was a heated one. Trotsky accused Stalin of having betrayed the Revolution. Stalin responded that its realization in praxis, that is the conquest and preservation of power, demonstrated the truth of his thought. Both were right and both were wrong. Those who fight the truth fight themselves.

What is certain is that in the twentieth century there are no other crimes comparable to Communism for the amount of time in which it spread, for the territories it embraced, for the amount and quality of hatred that it was able to secrete. But these crimes are consequences of errors. After the collapse of the Soviet Union these errors were as if released from the wrapping that contained them, to propagate like an ideological miasma over the entire West, under the form of cultural and moral relativism.

The relativism today professed and lived in the West is rooted in the theories of materialism and Marxist evolutionism; in other words, on the denial of any spiritual reality and any stable and permanent element in man and society.

19. Antonio Gramsci, *Quaderni dal Carcere* [*Prison Notebooks*], ed. Valentino Gerratana, vol. 3 (Einaudi, Torino 1975), 1860.

1517, 1717, 1917: Three Revolutions and Fatima

Antonio Gramsci is the theorist behind this cultural revolution that transforms the dictatorship of the proletariat into the dictatorship of relativism. The task of Communism, for Gramsci, is to bring to the people the integral secularism that the Enlightenment had reserved to a restricted élite. On the social level, this atheistic secularism is actuated, according to the words of the Italian Communist, by means of a "complete secularization of all life and all customs connected to it," that is, through an absolute secularization of social life, which will allow for the Communist "praxis" to extirpate the social roots of religion. The new Europe with no roots, which has expelled every reference to Christianity from its founding treatise, has fully realized the Gramscian plan for the secularization of society.

We need to acknowledge the fact that the Fatima prophecy, which said that Russia would scatter her errors throughout the world, has been fulfilled. The fall of the Iron Curtain made the diffusion of these errors unstoppable. The decomposition of Communism has putrefied the West. Anti-Communism, for its part, has vanished, because "very few have been able to penetrate the true nature of Communism," as Pius XI had warned in *Divini Redemptoris*. Nowadays, one feels almost embarrassed to say he is anti-Communist. This is Communism's great victory: that it is has gone down without the shedding of a drop of blood, without being put on trial, without an ideological indictment to condemn its memory.

In his book *Judgment in Moscow: Soviet Crimes and Western Complicity*, Vladimir Bukovsky wrote:

> Any event in our lives, even if it is of small significance, comes under the scrutiny of some commission or other. Especially if people have been killed. A plane crash, a railroad disaster, an industrial accident—and experts argue, conduct analyses, seek to determine the degree of guilt . . . even of governments if they had the slightest connection

with what occurred.... Yet here we have a conflict...
which affected practically every country in the world, cost
scores of millions in lives and hundreds of billions in dol-
lars, and—as has so often been claimed—almost brought
about global destruction, which is not being examined by
a single country or international organization.

Is it so surprising that alongside our willingness to
examine every accident, we refuse to investigate the greatest catastrophe of our time? For in our heart of hearts we
already know the conclusions such an investigation would
yield, as any sane person knows full well when he has
entered into collusion with evil. Even if the intellect pro-
vides speciously logical and outwardly acceptable excuses,
the voice of conscience whispers that our fall began from
the moment we agreed to "peaceful coexistence" with
evil.[20]

Unfortunately the Catholic Church has promoted, and is
promoting, this "peaceful coexistence" with evil.

When the communist dictator Fidel Castro died on
November 26, 2016, he received praise from the entire West
and even from the Catholic Church. Pope Francis, the seventh successor to Pius XI, in an interview given to Eugenio
Scalfari, compared Communism to Christianity and affirmed that inequalities are "the greatest evil that exists in
the world."[21] Yet the essence of Communism lies precisely in
the suppression of any form of social differences and the
religious expression of this egalitarianism is the ecumenical
equalization of all religions, just as its philosophical expression is ecological pantheism.

Pope Bergoglio recently received in the Vatican the exponents of the so-called "popular movements," representatives

20. Vladimir Bukovsky, *Gli archivi segreti di Mosca*, Italian trans. (Spi-
rali, Milano 1999), 62, 65.
21. *La Repubblica*, November 11, 2016.

of the new Marxist-ecologist left, and expressed his liking for the pro-Marxist regimes of the Castro brothers in Cuba, Chávez and Maduro in Venezuela, Morales in Bolivia, Rafael Correa in Ecuador, and José Mujica in Uruguay.

Cardinal Zen, the Bishop Emeritus of Hong Kong and China's highest-ranking prelate, in an interview accuses Pope Francis of "selling out" Chinese Catholics by striking a deal with the Communist government.[22]

The errors of Communism have not only been scattered throughout the world, but have penetrated into the temple of God, like the smoke of Satan enveloping and suffocating the Mystical Body of Christ.

The smoke of Satan in the Church

And it is not only this. At Fatima, Our Lady showed the three little shepherds the terrifying vision of hell where the souls of poor sinners go, and it was revealed to Jacinta that it was sins against purity that lead most souls to hell. Who could possibly have imagined one hundred years later that the public profession of impurity would have been added to the immense number of impure sins that are committed, under the form of sexual liberation and the introduction of extramarital unions, even homosexual, into the laws of the most important nations of the West?

And who could have ever imagined that a pontifical document—Pope Francis's Postsynodal Apostolic Exhortation *Amoris Laetitia,* issued on April 8, 2016—would endorse adultery? The divine and natural law does not admit exceptions. Those who allow the exception destroy the rule. In one of the *dubia* addressed by the cardinals to the pope we read: "After *Amoris Laetitia* n. 301, is it still possible to

22. *LifeSiteNews,* February 22, 2017.

affirm that a person who habitually lives in contradiction to a commandment of God's law, as for instance the one that prohibits adultery (cf. Mt 19:3–9), finds him or herself in an objective situation of grave habitual sin?" The fact that today a doubt of this sort can be presented to the pope and the Congregation for the Doctrine of the Faith indicates how very grave and deep is the crisis in which the Church is immersed.

Cardinal Kasper and other pastors and theologians have stated that the Church must adapt its evangelical message to the praxis of the times. But the primacy of praxis over doctrine is the heart of Marxism-Leninism. And if Marx stated that the task of philosophers is not to know the world but to transform it, today many theologians and pastors maintain that the task of theologians is not that of spreading the Truth, but of re-interpreting it in praxis. We need not then reform the habits of Christians in order to bring them back to Gospel teachings, but instead we should adapt the Gospel to the heteropraxis of Christians.

In the end my Immaculate Heart will triumph

The antidote to the dictatorship of relativism is the doctrinal and moral purity of the Immaculate Heart of Mary. It will be Our Lady, and not men, who will destroy the errors that threaten us. Heaven, though, has asked for mankind's concrete collaboration.

Our Lady states that the conditions to avoid chastisement are as follows: a public and solemn act of the consecration of Russia to her Immaculate Heart, done by the pope in union with all the bishops of the world, and the practice of reparatory Communion on the first Saturdays of the month.

The Second Vatican Ecumenical Council would have been a great opportunity to fulfill Our Lady's requests. In 1965, 510 archbishops and bishops from 78 countries signed a petition in which they asked the pope in union with the council fathers to consecrate the whole world to the Immaculate Heart of Mary, and in a special way Russia and the other nations dominated by Communism. Paul VI, however, paid no heed to the request.[23]

Pius XII and John Paul II made partial acts of consecration of Russia or of the world: fruitful, not lacking in effects, but incomplete.

On May 12, 2010, Benedict XVI, in the Chapel of the Apparitions at Fatima, raised a prayer of entrustment to Our Lady, asking for our liberation from "every danger threatening us." But this act also was incomplete.

Those devoted to Fatima hoped for something more from Pope Francis, compared to his predecessors, but were disappointed. In his Act of Entrustment to Mary made on October 13, 2013, the pope did not mention the Immaculate Heart, nor the world, nor the Church, let alone Russia. Pope Francis went to Fatima on May 13, 2017. Again, he failed to comply with the requests of the Mother of God.

Today the consecration of Russia has still not been done, the practice of reparatory Communion on the First Saturdays is not being spread, and above all the atmosphere in which we are immersed is a spirit of degenerate hedonism, in the satisfaction of every pleasure and desire, outside the moral law. Who could claim, then, that the prophecy of Fatima has been fulfilled and that the great events preannounced by Our Lady in 1917 are behind us?

Our Lady at Fatima did not only ask the hierarchy of the Church for public acts. Along with these necessary actions there has to be a profound spirit of interior conversion and

---

23. Archbishop Geraldo de Proença Sigaud personally delivered the petition to Paul VI; see Roberto de Mattei, *The Second Vatican Council: An Unwritten Story* (Loreto Publications, Fitzwilliam 2012), 339. The full text of the petition may be found in the Brazilian magazine *Catolicismo*, n. 159 (1964).

penance, as we are reminded in the Third Secret, in the triple call of the angel for penance.

Penance signifies above all repentance, a spirit of contrition, which makes us aware of the gravity of sins committed by us and others, and which makes us detest them with all our hearts. Penance signifies a doctrinal and moral revision of all the errors embraced in the last century by Western society. The Fatima message reminds us explicitly that the alternative to penance is a terrifying punishment that threatens mankind.

For the world to avoid this punishment it must change its spirit, but it cannot do so if it will not recognize the enormity of the sins that are committed, starting with the introduction of the mass-murder of the unborn and homosexual unions into laws. These both represent sins directly against God, Creator of nature: sins, as the Catechism teaches, that cry out to Heaven for vengeance; in other words, they incur a great chastisement.

Without repentance, the chastisement cannot be held back. Without reference to this chastisement, the message of Fatima is emptied of its deep significance.

Penance signifies repentance; penance signifies detestation and hatred of sin. The hatred of sin must impel us to fight it, and when the sin is public it must impel us toward public action, to combat the roots and the consequences of the evil in society. Thus the call to penance in the Fatima message is also a call to combat the errors that are corrupting the whole of society today.

The Fatima message is not only an anti-Communist message; it is also an anti-liberal and anti-Lutheran message, as the errors of Russia descend from the errors of the French Revolution and Protestantism. They are the errors of the anti-Christian revolution, which the Catholic counter-revolution opposes. As Count de Maistre states, the Catholic counter-revolution is not a revolution against the Revolution, but rather it is opposition to the Revolution in all its political, cultural, and religious aspects.[24] Fatima directly opposes 1917, 1717, and 1517. We will not be celebrating any of these anniversaries.

Allow me to recall a revelation from Our Lady at Fatima that we learned about only a few years ago, in 2013 when the Carmel of Coimbra published the volume *Um Caminho sob o olhar de Maria*. Around four in the afternoon on January 3, 1944, in the convent chapel of Tuy, in front of the Tabernacle, Our Lady urged Sister Lucia to write the text of the Third Secret, and Sister Lucia recounts:

> I felt my spirit inundated by a mystery of light that is God and in Him I saw and heard the point of a lance like a flame that is detached touch the axis of the earth and it trembles: mountains, cities, towns, and villages with their inhabitants are buried. The sea, the rivers and clouds exceed their boundaries, inundating and dragging with them in a vortex houses and people in a number that cannot be counted; it is the purification of the world from the sin in which it is immersed. Hatred, ambition, provoke the destructive war. Afterward I felt my heart racing and in my spirit a soft voice that said: "In time, one faith, one baptism, one Church, Holy, Catholic, Apostolic. In eternity, Heaven!" This word *Heaven* filled my heart with peace and happiness in such a way that, almost without being aware of it, I kept repeating to myself for a long time: Heaven, Heaven![25]

Our Lady reminds us that a dreadful chastisement threatens mankind and that profession of the Catholic faith in its entirety is necessary in the dramatic age we are living in. One Faith, one Baptism, and one Church. We must not then leave the Church, but turn back to her and live and die in her, since

---

24. Joseph de Maistre, *Considérations sur la France*, ch. X, 3, in *Œuvres complètes* (Vitte, Lyon-Paris 1924), 1:157.

25. Carmel of Coimbra, *Um Caminho sob o olhar de Maria* (Ediçoes Carmelo, Coimbra 2012), 267.

outside the Church there is no salvation. Outside her doors there is only the inconsolable abyss of hell. The alternative remains as it has always been: Heaven or Hell, which have their own foretastes on this earth. Hell for the nations is an atheistic, anarchistic, egalitarian society. Paradise for the nations is an austere, hierarchical, sacred, Christian Civilization.

We conquer for Heaven on earth by fighting in defense of the true Church, so often abandoned by churchmen. And the final exclamation, "Heaven! Heaven!," seems to refer to the dramatic choice between Heaven, the place where souls that are saved reach eternal happiness, and hell, the place where the damned undergo sufferings for all eternity.

Those who want to escape death, in time and eternity, have only one path before them: to fight against the disorders in the modern world; to affirm, in their lives and in society, the perennial principles of the natural and Christian order. This was the path chosen by many saints who should be our models, such as St. Maximilian Kolbe (1894–1941). On October 17, 1917, on the eve of the Russian Revolution and without knowing anything about the apparitions at Fatima, the young Polish Franciscan founded the Militia of the Immaculata to combat Freemasonry, which was celebrating the two-hundredth anniversary of the constitution of London's Grand Lodge with blasphemous parades through the streets of Rome. St. Maximilian Kolbe is one of the saints who prophesied the Triumph of the Immaculate Heart of Mary. The Triumph of Mary's Immaculate Heart, which is also the Reign of Mary announced by many privileged souls, is nothing other than the triumph in history of the natural and Christian order, preserved by the Church. Our Lady announced this triumph as the final outcome of a long trial, of tragic days of penance and struggle, but also of immense trust in her promise.

Let us turn to her then, in this centenary year of her apparitions, asking her to make haste, at this moment, to make each of us an instrument in our times for her victory against the Revolution: *super revolutionem victoria in diebus nostris,* which is equivalent to saying: in the end her Immaculate Heart will triumph.

1918 and 1968:
Irruptions of Disorder and
the Catholic Response[1]

THE CHURCH is the Mystical Body of Christ: a reality that transcends history, but in history lives and battles and hence is called the Church Militant. For this reason we cannot speak about the Church without reflecting on the historical horizon in which she operates. In 2017, we commemorated three revolutions that changed the course of history: the Protestant Revolution, the French Revolution, and the Communist Revolution—three revolutions that are part of a single revolutionary process.[2]

2018 is the anniversary of two events positioned inside the same revolutionary process: the hundred years since the end of the First World War and the fifty years since the Revolution of 1968. These anniversaries help us to place the crisis of the Church in its historical context.

The First World War shook up the political geography of Europe. The disappearance of the Austrian Empire deprived the European continent of its center of gravity, paving the way for the Second World War. But the postwar period of the early twentieth century was principally a revolution in the culture and mentality of European man. It was the end of an era.

---

1. A lecture given at the Una Voce Canada Annual General Meeting, Holy Family Parish, Vancouver, British Columbia, November 10, 2018.

2. See the preceding lecture, and Plinio Corrêa de Oliveira, *Revolution and Counter-Revolution.*

Irruptions of Disorder and the Catholic Response

We ought to reread the memoirs of the Austrian writer Stefan Zweig (1881–1942): *Die Welt von Gestern* [The World of Yesterday]. Zweig writes in this book:

> If I try to come up with a convenient formula to describe the time preceding the First World War—the period I grew up in—I believe the most concise possible would be to say that it was the age of certainty. In our Austrian monarchy that lasted almost for a millennium, everything seemed to be eternal and the state itself appeared to be the supreme guarantee of this continuity.... Everything in the solid Empire appeared to be sound and immovable, and in the highest position there was the venerable old Sovereign.... No one was thinking about wars, revolutions, and upheavals. Any radical act, any violence, appeared then to be impossible in the age of reason.[3]

Everything appeared eternal, sound, immovable. However, behind those stable and apparently indestructible institutions on which society was based, from the family to the monarchy, there was a conception of the world founded upon an order of unchangeable values. The guardian of these absolute values was, and still is, the Catholic Church.

Stability, order, equilibrium are all good things, but there is not one good thing in this world that does not come from the Church, the only divine institution, always perfect, no matter how imperfect the men who represent her can be.

On the eve of the First World War, the men who were at the helm of the Barque of Peter were two saints: Pius X and his Secretary of State, Rafael Merry del Val. St. Pius X died a month after the start of the war and understood its catastrophic significance.

During the First World War the Russian Revolution broke out. It was the matrix for all the other social and political

---

3. Stefan Zweig, *Die Welt von Gestern. Erinnerungen eines Europäers.* Italian trans. *Il mondo di ieri* (Arnoldo Mondadori, Milan 1994), 9, 27–28.

revolutions that came after. The totalitarianisms of the twentieth century destroyed the old order, but they did not build a new order. The essence of totalitarianism is not the hypertrophy of the state, as many believe, but the destruction of the natural social order. Totalitarianism dissolves, in effect, all principles and institutions and renders man destitute of any social protection—to achieve the dictatorship of chaos. Political, intellectual, and moral disorder was the common thread of the twentieth century—the century of revolutions, world wars, and genocides, the bloodiest century in Western history.[4]

The '68 Revolution was a revolution that did not shed blood like those before, but it shed something much worse: it shed the tears of a generation that lost not only its bodies but also its souls. Sixty-Eight was the most devastating of all the preceding revolutions because it enthroned chaos in the everyday life of Western man.

From a fluid society to a fluid Church

In attempting to define our age, sociologists like Zygmunt Baumann speak of a "fluid society" in which all forms are dissolved, even basic ones of social aggregation. The "fluid life" that Baumann writes about is the precarious and ephemeral life of modern man: a life devoid of roots and foundations, as he lives only for the present, immersed in the liquefaction of all values and institutions. Everything that is liquidated is consumed—or, we might say, everything that is consumed is liquidated: from food products to individual lives.[5] Everything is fluid, since everything changes, everything is in a state of becoming. In philosophical terms

---

4. Robert Conquest, *Reflections on a Ravaged Century.*

5. Zygmunt Baumann, *La vita liquida*, Italian translation (Laterza, Rome 2006), ix.

we might define our society as based on the triumph of pure becoming, the most radical negation of the primacy of Being that has ever existed in history.

The fluid society cannot be compared to a river that flows, since the river comes from a living source and has a destination: the immense sea that awaits it. The fluid society has no destination: it just erodes the rock. Yet it only erodes the surfaces and dissolves the incrustations, and everything is transformed into mud. Rock in its essence is indestructible. Nothing can be done against the force of being.

The first name of God is Being, as God Himself revealed to Moses at the burning bush (Ex 3:14). All the divine attributes flow from this Being as from a primordial spring. Every perfection in reality comes down to a grade of being that refers back to an absolute Being, without limit and without conditions.

This philosophical primacy of Being has been taught by the Church ever since its birth. The Church has a doctrine and a law that are absolute and immutable, reflecting the eternal law, which is God. This law and this doctrine are contained in Holy Scripture and in Tradition; the role of the Magisterium is to preserve these and to hand them on. Not one iota of these principles can be changed. Of course, throughout history, Christians may have distanced themselves from the truth and from the precepts of the Church in their personal lives. These are the epochs of decadence that demand a profound reform, i.e., a return to observance of abandoned principles. If this does not happen, then the temptation is to transform immoral behavior into principles opposed to Christian truths. This temptation penetrated the Church during the Second Vatican Council and is now proposed to us via the concept of the primacy of pastoral practice.

The spirit of the Second Vatican Council

The Second Vatican Council was a cultural revolution that preceded the one of 1968. The slogan that sums up the spirit of '68 is "It is forbidden to forbid" (*Il est interdit d'interdire*). Every affirmation, in effect, if it is clear, firm, and categorical, entails the negation of the opposite affirmation. To forbid to forbid means that there are no categorical affirmations, absolute rules, or non-negotiable principles. Man does not act by following rules, but by obeying impulses, sentiments, and desires.

This idea was formulated for the first time by John XXIII in his allocution that opened Vatican II on October 11, 1962. Pope John explained that the council had been launched not to condemn errors or formulate new dogmas, but rather to propose, with language adapted to new times, the perennial teaching of the Church.[6] We are told that Church doctrine does not change, but only the way in which this doctrine is communicated. What actually happened was that the primacy attributed to the pastoral dimension effected a revolution in language, in mentality, and in the life of the Church.

The slogan of the Second Vatican Council was: it is forbidden to condemn, since condemnation is a negative attitude, which results in aggressive reactions in the one that is condemned. To forbid condemnation means that there is no need to fight evil, for if we do then evil will fight us. A slogan that anticipated—not followed—Vatican II.

According to the progressive theologians, the cause of the rejection of the Church and of the anticlericalism of the nineteenth and twentieth centuries was the intolerant atti-

---

6. John XXIII, Allocution *Gaudet Mater Ecclesiae* of October 11, 1962, in AAS 54 (1962), 792.

tude of the Church toward her enemies. The transition to a new kind of pastoral care would appease enemies, and would open up a new era of peace and collaboration of the world with the Church. The appeasing coexistence of *Ostpolitik,* which sought in the past to compromise with Communism, and today's agreement with Communist China, originate from this pastoral revolution. The outcome, nonetheless, was not a decrease but an exponential increase of anti-Christianity in the world. The Church, in her visible structures, lost her militant identity and has been liquefied.

Pastoral care is that which, through updating (*aggiornamento*), is modified and transformed continuously. The primacy of the pastoral signifies a "fluidization" of the principles and institutions of the Church. The solid, permanent Church with a backbone has been replaced by a "fluid" Church, like the society in which we live. This new Church is based on the primacy of becoming over Being and of evolution over Tradition.

Principles, truths, certainties are solid because they constitute a channel that ensures the waters of the river are not dispersed; they are a dam that ensures the lake will not overflow. If the dam fails, society will be flooded by the water.

According to Father Roger-Thomas Calmel:

> Doctrines, rites, and the interior life are [now] subjected to a process of such a radical and refined liquefaction that it no longer allows for a distinction between Catholics and non-Catholics. Because 'yes' and 'no,' the definite and the definitive are considered outdated, the question arises as to what it is that impedes non-Christian religions from also being part of the new universal church, constantly updated by ecumenical interpretations.[7]

This is the spirit of Vatican II.

---

7. Roger T. Calmel, O.P., *Breve apologia della chiesa di sempre,* 10–11.

Revolution and Tradition

This process, the liquefying of the Church and society, is a revolutionary project that started a long time ago.

We know the Permanent Instruction of the *Alta Vendita*, a secret document written in the early nineteenth century that mapped out a blueprint for the subversion of the Catholic Church. The entire world has witnessed a profound change within the Catholic Church on an international scale, a change that is in step with the modern world.[8]

The anti-Christian revolution that runs through history bears a hatred for Being in all its expressions. Opposed to Being, it rejects all that is stable, permanent, and objective in reality, starting with human nature. The Church, family, private property, and the state are denied at their roots because social institutions rooted in human nature are said not to exist: everything is the product of a historical process. Man himself is said to lack any true nature: man is amorphous matter that can be pressed into shape and adapted at will. "Gender theory" is a product of this evolutionary vision, according to which man has neither nature nor essence of his own.

The only alternative to the nihilist revolution that is today attacking not only the Church but also the natural order— not only the natural order but even human nature itself—is to rediscover the fullness of Being in all its forms. To do this is also to rediscover the stability and permanence of the real in all its forms, both individual and social. We must oppose the fluid conception of the world, based on the primacy of becoming, with an axiological vision based on the primacy of Being.

Axiology is the science of values. Value is "that through

---

8. John Vennari, *The Permanent Instruction of the Alta Vendita* (Fatima Center, Buffalo [N.Y.] 2018).

which a thing has worth." Value is therefore that which gives reality its significance and its perfection. Values are principles whose perfection is rooted in the supreme principle of all reality. Above all principles there is a universal principle, which is the center and source of all laws without exception. This is God, the most perfect Being, the first principle, the First Truth, as St. Thomas defined Him,[9] on which the ultimate principles, absolute values, and universal truths are based. Only God does not change, and only that which is based in God and dwells in Him deserves to be preserved, handed on, and looked after.

The Church, immutable in her divine constitution, her doctrine and rites, is the image on earth of the perfection of Being. And in the Church the reflection of the Divine Being is her Tradition. Tradition is that which is stable in the eternal becoming of things. It is that which does not change in a world that changes, and it is this because it is a reflection of eternity.

The Church's Tradition, like Holy Scripture, is a source of Revelation, divinely assisted by the Holy Spirit. Tradition is the word of Jesus Christ teaching his Apostles before and after his Passion, death, and Resurrection. In the forty days between the Resurrection and the Ascension, He appeared several times to his Mother and to the Apostles and explained clearly, and in detail, the sense of the mission of the Church He had founded. He explained the significance of the Last Supper and of the Divine Sacrifice they had to perpetuate. The first Mass, celebrated by St. Peter, followed meticulously the instructions of Christ and has been handed down to us in that rite which we call traditional.

We know that Divine Revelation concluded with the death of the last Apostle, St. John. However, this revelation is not contained only in the four Gospels and in Holy Scrip-

---

9. *Summa Theologiae*, II-II, q. 1, a. 1.

ture, but also in the teachings the Apostles received from Christ's own lips. We can imagine to what extent Our Lady preserved and memorized all these truths and these rites in her pure Heart, and with what faithfulness she then passed them on to the Apostles. St. John was not only the last to hand on in person the words he had heard; he was also, through his intimacy with Our Lady, perhaps the one who received to the greatest extent the light of Tradition. He died at the end of the first century, and only a few years after his death the *lex orandi* and the *lex credendi* of the Church had been immutably defined.

In the course of the following centuries, the Church would explain, clarify, and define these truths. But she never innovated or transformed them. The mission of the Church is to keep custody of Tradition, to defend it and to hand it on. There is a relationship, which Father Calmel has brought to light, between, on the one hand, the immutable and permanent nature of the Church, and, on the other hand, human nature, which is equally stable and objective. It is not just the perfection of its divine origin "that makes the Church definitive and unchangeable," says Father Calmel. "It is also the stability of the characteristics of the human race that the Church has the mission and the power to enlighten and to save."[10] Stability of rites in defense of the sacraments; stability of the dogmatic formulae in defense of revealed truths; stability of the *lex orandi* and of the *lex credendi*.

Tradition is not only the *regula fidei*, the rule of the Faith of the Church; it is also the foundation of society. The Church, indeed, is our leader not only in faith but also in morals. The morality of a society is expressed in practices, customs, and habits, that is, in a historic and concrete tradition that reflects divine and natural tradition. Tradition

10. R. T. Calmel, O.P., *Brève apologie pour l'Eglise de toujours* (Editions Difralivre, Maule 1987), 23.

judges history not in the name of history itself but instead in the name of the truths that transcend it.

In this world, whether we are speaking of moral life or of physical life, there are some things that pass away and other things that remain. Tradition is the incorruptible and immutable element of society. Tradition is that which does not pass away. And it is only within Tradition that progress is possible, because we cannot progress or improve ourselves by means of things that pass away. We can do so only in things that remain. Tradition is that of the past that lives in the present; it is that which must live in order for our present to have a future. It is the ultimate root of all that is, and of all that will be. It is God Himself, in Whom past, present, and future are grounded in a single and infinite act of being.

Tradition and sensus fidei

What encourages our conscience, enlightened by the eternal and immutable Magisterium of the Church, is Tradition—that Tradition which is no remote rule but rather something we need to hold on to closely, especially when we see that the present living Magisterium is so vacillating. In the Church, indeed, the ultimate rule of faith during periods when people desert it is not the contemporary living Magisterium, in its non-definitive aspects, but instead the eternal Magisterium that, together with Holy Scripture, constitutes one of the sources by which we know the Word of God.[11]

There is nothing subjective or Protestant in this position. What subjectivists and Protestants do is to replace the Magisterium of the Church with a different magisterium. They deny the Church's right to teach the truth and they replace the truths taught by the Church with their own truths. There is none of this in our approach. We do not claim to replace

11. See above, pp. 131 ff.; cf. R. de Mattei, *Apologia della Tradizione.*

the Magisterium of the Church with any other magisterium. We see ourselves as simple members of the learning Church, *ecclesia discens*, simple faithful who believe that the teaching Church alone, *ecclesia docens*, has the right and duty to teach.

The expression "simple faithful" contains the little—but also the lot—that we are. The learning Church is not the teaching Church but just always the Church, assisted by the Holy Spirit. As simple faithful, we are members of the Mystical Body: while we do not have the right to teach, we have the right to ask our pastors to confirm us in the Faith.

We are guided in this by our conscience, which is not subjective but instead is rooted in faith. Our conscience tells us not to retreat, but instead to raise the banner of Tradition. One becomes part of the Church by means of the Sacrament of Baptism, which is fulfilled in the Sacrament of Confirmation. Through Baptism we enter the Church Militant; but it is Confirmation that makes us true soldiers of Christ. Baptism instills the faith, Confirmation requires us to profess it and defend it in public. Baptism and Confirmation instill in us the *sensus fidei*, which is the shared awareness of the faithful. This is adherence to the truths of the Faith by supernatural instinct more than by theological reasoning.

Tradition is maintained and transmitted by the Church not only through the Magisterium but through all the faithful, "from the bishops down to the laity," as the famous formula by St. Augustine expresses. The doctor from Hippo makes an appeal in particular to "the people of the Faith" who do not exercise a Magisterium, but on the basis of their *sensus fidei* guarantee the continuity of the transmission of a truth.[12]

The *sensus fidei* plays a decisive role during times of crisis in which an evident contradiction between the subjective Magisterium and the objective one is created, between the authorities that teach and the truths of the faith they must

12. St. Augustine, *De praedestinatione sanctorum*, 14, 27, PL 44:980.

guard and transmit. The *sensus fidei* induces the believer to reject any ambiguity and falsification of the truth, leaning on the immutable Tradition of the Church, which does not oppose the Magisterium but includes it.

Cardinal Walter Brandmüller, speaking in Rome on April 7, 2018, recalled how "the *'sensus fidei'* acts as a sort of spiritual immune system, through which the faithful instinctively recognize or reject any error. Upon this *'sensus fidei'* rests then—apart from the divine promise—also the passive infallibility of the Church, or the certainty that the Church, in her totality, shall never be able to incur a heresy."

It was the *sensus fidei* that guided faithful Catholics during the Arian crisis of the fourth century. It was then that St. Jerome coined the phrase wherein "the whole world groaned and woke astounded to find itself Arian."[13] What is important to underline is that this was not merely a doctrinal dispute limited to some theologians, nor a simple clash between bishops where the pope had to act as an arbiter. It was a religious war in which all Christians were involved, from the pope down to the least of the faithful. Nobody closed themselves up in a spiritual bunker, nobody stood looking out the window, a mute spectator of the drama. Everyone was down in the trenches fighting on one side of the battle lines.

It was not easy at that time to understand whether your own bishop was orthodox or not, but the *sensus fidei* was the compass by which to orient oneself. Saint Hilary writes that during the Arian crisis the ears of the faithful who interpreted in an orthodox sense the ambiguous affirmations of the Semi-Arian theologians were holier than the lips of the priests. The Christians who for three centuries had resisted emperors were now resisting their own shepherds, in some cases even the pope—guilty, if not of open heresy, at least of grave negligence.

13. St. Jerome, *Dialogus adversus Luciferianos*, n. 19, PL 23:171.

There are times when a Catholic is obliged to choose between cowardice and heroism, between apostasy and holiness. This is what happened in the fourth century and it is happening even today. Cardinal Willem Jacobus Eijk, Archbishop of Utrecht, summarized the matter in his statement of May 7, 2018, in these words: "The bishops and, above all, the Successor of Peter are failing to maintain and transmit faithfully the deposit of faith."[14] These are very strong words that directly call into question the conduct of the successor of Peter, Pope Francis.

A situation without precedent in history. Yet, while the history of the Church is always new, it is always repeating itself. It is always new because the external persecutions and internal crises she endures change: they have different motivations, different protagonists, different magnitudes, and different intensities. But in these crises, no matter how deep they can be, there is something that does not change: the force of Tradition, which is destined to defeat any revolution that opposes it.

The success and failure of the Revolution

The philosophy of the Revolution is the philosophy of pure becoming. A becoming that, as it is unmoored from Being, flows irreversibly towards the void, towards nothingness, and thus self-destructs. This is the path the Revolution takes.

In fact, revolution, like evil, does not have its own nature, but exists only insofar as it is the privation and a deficiency of good. "The being of evil," explains Saint Thomas, "consists precisely in being the privation of good."[15] Evil, which is the privation of being, can spread like darkness in the night, following daylight. But the darkness does not have in itself the power to defeat the light in a total and definitive way,

14. Published online at *National Catholic Register,* May 7, 2018.
15. *Summa Theologiae,* I, q. 14, a. 10, resp.

because darkness draws its existence from the light. Infinite light, which is God, exists. "God is light, and in Him there is no darkness," says Saint John (1 John 1:5). Absolute darkness does not exist, because radical nothingness cannot exist. Our existence is the living negation of nothingness. Evil advances when good recedes. Error is affirmed only when the truth is extinguished. Revolution wins only when Tradition surrenders. All revolutions throughout history have taken place only when an authentic opposition is lacking.

However, if there is an evil dynamic, there is also a dynamic of goodness. A remnant—however minimal—of light cannot be extinguished, and this remnant has in itself the irresistible strength of daybreak, the possibility of a new day with the sunrise. This is the drama of evil: it cannot destroy the last remnant of good that survives; it is destined to be destroyed by this remnant. Evil cannot stand even the smallest surviving good, because it glimpses its defeat in the good that exists. The dynamism of evil is destined to shatter itself against that which stays, which remains solid in spite of society's liquefaction. Therefore, the final step in the process of today's self-dissolution eroding the rock on which the Church was founded is destined to witness the death of the Revolution and the sprouting of the beginning of an opposed life: a mandatory itinerary of restoration of faith and morals, of truth and of the social order to which it corresponds: this principle is the Catholic counter-revolution.

Thus what is irreversible is not the triumph of the Revolution but rather its defeat. And this will happen thanks to the dynamism of the good, which opposes the dynamism of evil in history.

Revolution is in fact a parasite that lives and maintains itself on the remnants of the true and the good that survive in the order it wants to destroy. These remnants, although minimal, always constitute a seed of potential multiplication and diffusion, whereas revolution is, of its very nature, sterile and infertile. And if revolution is unable to annihilate order, this means that its dynamism is intended to break against a remnant of the truth and goodness that constitute the principle and presupposition of its defeat.

The Revolution of 1968 was successful because its creators occupied key roles in politics, the mass media, and culture: it was successful because it changed the West's mentality and way of life.

Nevertheless, the Revolution of '68 failed because it was born of a protest against a one-dimensional society, the bourgeois society of comfort and wealth; but the society that Sixty-Eight produced—contemporary society—is the society *par excellence* for consumerism and hedonism; it is a relativist society in which all the flames of idealism have been snuffed out. Today reality is interpreted as a system of power that is primarily economic, not value-based. Power—power without truth—is the only value of our time. All values, the philosopher Augusto Del Noce points out, are destined to be incorporated into the category of vitality. But a society that is unaware of any principle other than that of purely expanding its own vaguely-defined vitality can only dissolve.[16]

The Revolution of '68 also failed because its slogan was "it is forbidden to forbid." However, contemporary society is a dictatorship unprecedented in history; the dictatorship of relativism, a psychological and moral dictatorship, which does not destroy the body but isolates, discriminates, and kills the soul of those who resist it.

In a similar way, the revolution in the Church had success because the progressive theologians of Vatican II and their heirs are governing the Church today; it has been a success because it has transformed the Catholic way of believing, praying, and loving.

---

16. Augusto Del Noce, in AA. VV., *La crisi della società permissiva* (Ares, Milan 1972).

Irruptions of Disorder and the Catholic Response

On the other hand, the revolution in the Church has failed because it was presented as a great pastoral reform and instead has resulted in the corruption of faith and morals: an unparalleled corruption, which has reached the point of enthroning homosexuality among the highest level of the ecclesiastical hierarchy. It has failed because its slogan was "it is forbidden to forbid," which did not result in greater freedom in the Church but in a dictatorial regime, hitherto unknown, so much so that a Catholic historian, Henry Sire, has described Pope Francis as *The Dictator Pope*.[17]

In my view, Pope Francis's pontificate is at an impasse. The contradiction that he is faced with is this: in order to ensure that the Revolution prevails in the Church he should exercise infallibility. But he cannot do it, because the Holy Spirit will not allow it; and he doesn't want to do it, because any defining act that he makes would be a contradiction of the primacy of the pastoral over doctrine, which he upholds. Pope Francis cannot replace the sword of truth with that of error, since the heirs of Vatican II have replaced the battle with ecumenism. The Church of Tradition, on the other hand, has not given up the battle, has not given up brandishing the sword of truth; and the first act of a pope of Tradition—who will be elected one day—will be that of exercising the *munus* of infallibility to define solemnly the truths that today are denied and to condemn the errors widespread in the Church today with the same solemnity.

The hour of victory

Certainly the blessed hour of victory will be preceded by a great chastisement, because the contemporary world has not followed the example of the inhabitants of Nineveh, who

17. Marcantonio Colonna (Henry Sire), *The Dictator Pope: The Inside Story of the Francis Papacy* (Regnery Publishing, Washington 2017).

were converted and saved, but rather that of the inhabitants of Sodom and Gomorrah, who refused to convert and were annihilated. The theology of history tells us that God rewards and punishes not only individual people but also collectives and social groups: families, nations, civilizations. But while individuals have their reward or their chastisement sometimes on earth but always in eternity, nations— which do not have eternal life—are punished or rewarded only on earth.

The revolutionary process consists in a plot of offenses against God that, linked together over the course of centuries, form one single collective sin, an apostasy of peoples and nations. And because each sin has a corresponding chastisement, the Christian theology of history teaches us that collective sins are followed by great historical catastrophes, which serve to pay for the public sins of nations. In these catastrophes the justice of God is never separated from His mercy, and because the mercy of God is linked to repentance, chastisement becomes inevitable when the world, by refusing repentance and penance, calls down upon itself not mercy but the justice of God. God, however, does not cease to be infinitely merciful, but at the same time He is infinitely just, and the theology of history shows us that from the creation of the universe to the end of the world there have been and will be immense sins that are followed by acts of the immense mercy of God.

The sin of revolution, which in the course of the centuries thwarted the development of Christian civilization and has led us to the spiritual and moral ruin of our time, cannot but arouse a reaction that, sustained by divine grace, will lead to the historical fulfillment of the great plan of Divine Providence.

We are the defenders of Tradition and two virtues are required of us: fortitude and confidence. Fortitude is the virtue of those who resist and do not retreat; confidence is the virtue of those who hope in the victory promised at Fatima by Our Lady herself to the Catholic faithful. The militant spirit of those who resist and trust must characterize our battle.

The heart of Tradition is in God, whose very essence is immutable and eternal Being. It is in God, and only in God, and in her who is His perfect echo, the Blessed Virgin Mary, that the defenders of the Faith and Tradition can find the necessary supernatural strength to brave the current crisis.

We are warriors without power. Warriors without weapons, faced with an enormous Goliath. And, from a human point of view, without power, without weapons, a battle cannot be won. Nevertheless God is pleased with our weakness and asks of us only a militant spirit. It will be God, through the Blessed Virgin Mary, Who gives us the weapons and the power to fight a battle that is not ours, but His. And God always wins—in time and in eternity.

Postscript

"It is not possible to unite what is contradictory"
Aldo Maria Valli Interviews Roberto de Mattei [1]

*P*ROFESSOR DE MATTEI, *not a day passes without this pontificate causing new confusion and doubts for many of the faithful. The declaration about other religions made at Abu Dhabi has provoked a great amount of concern. It seems there is no way of avoiding the fact that it is problematic. How do you interpret it?*

The Abu Dhabi declaration made on February 4, 2019, signed by Pope Francis and the grand imam of Al-Azhar, affirms that "the pluralism and the diversity of religions, color, sex, race and language are willed by God in His wisdom, through which He created human beings." This affirmation contradicts the teaching of the Church, which says the one true religion is the Catholic religion. In fact, it is only by faith in Jesus Christ and in His Name that men can attain eternal salvation (cf. Acts 4:12).

On March 1, during the *ad limina* visit of the bishops of Kazakhstan to Rome, Bishop Athanasius Schneider expressed his perplexity to Pope Francis about the Abu Dhabi declaration. The pope replied to him that "the diversity of religions is only the permissive will of God." This answer

1. This interview was published in Italian by Aldo Maria Valli (www.aldomariavalli.it) on April 3, 2019, and in the present translation by Giuseppe Pellegrino on April 4 at OnePeterFive (www.onepeterfive.com).

Postscript

is deceptive, because while it seems to admit that the plurality of religions is an evil permitted by God but not willed by him, the same is not true of the diversity of sexes and races, which are positively willed by God. When Bishop Schneider expressed this objection, Pope Francis admitted that the phrase "could be understood erroneously." Yet the pope never corrected or rectified his affirmation, and in fact the Pontifical Council for Interreligious Dialogue, at the Holy Father's request, directed all bishops to see to the widespread diffusion of the Abu Dhabi declaration so that it "may become an object of research and reflection in all schools, universities and institutes of education and formation."

The interpretation thus being spread is that the plurality of religions is a good thing, not an evil that is merely tolerated by God. It seems to me that these deliberate contradictions are a microcosm of the entire pontificate of Pope Bergoglio.

How would you, as a historian of the Church, summarize the past six years?

As years of hypocrisy and lies. Jorge Mario Bergoglio was chosen because he appeared to be a bishop who was "humble and profoundly spiritual" (thus did Andrea Tornielli salute him in *La Stampa*), one "who would reform and purify the Church." But none of this happened. The pope did not remove the most corrupt prelates either from the Roman Curia or from individual dioceses. He has done so only when, as in the McCarrick case, he was forced to by public opinion. In reality, Francis has revealed himself to be a political pope, the most political pope of the last century. His political persuasion is that of left-wing Peronism, which detests, in principle, every form of inequality and is opposed to Western culture and society. When transferred into the ecclesiastical realm, Peronism joins with liberation theology and leads to an effort to impose synodal democratization on the Church, which strips her of her essential nature.

The summit on sexual abuse [held at the Vatican, February 21–24, 2019] seems as though it has already been forgotten. It was full of nice-sounding expressions that the mainstream media trumpeted, but it did not lead to anything new. In general, how do you judge the way in which the Holy See is addressing this crisis?

In a clearly contradictory way. The anti-abuse norms that have just been approved by Pope Francis circumvent the real problem, which is the relationship between the tribunals of the Church and the civil courts, or, seen more broadly, the relationship between the Church and the world. The Church has the right and duty to investigate and judge those who are accused of crimes that violate not only civil laws but also ecclesiastical laws established by canon law. In this case, it is necessary to open a regular penal trial in a Church tribunal that respects the fundamental rights of the accused and is not conditioned by the results of any civil trial.

Today, instead, in the case of Cardinal Pell, the Vatican has said it will open a canonical trial, but first it needs to "wait for the outcome of the [civil] appeals process." In the case of Cardinal Barbarin of France, condemned to six months in prison with probation and also awaiting an appeals process, there has similarly been no announcement of any canonical trial. When Cardinal Luis Francisco Ladaria, prefect of the Congregation for the Doctrine of the Faith, was called to testify in the Barbarin case by the judges in Lyon, the Vatican invoked diplomatic immunity, but it did not do this for Cardinal Pell. This policy of different standards for different people is part of the climate of ambiguity and duplicity we are living in.

Postscript

During this pontificate, new norms have been introduced for monastic life, and in particular for the cloister. Some monastic communities are very worried, because they consider these new norms a threat to contemplative life. Do you share this concern?

Yes, it seems as though there is a plan to destroy contemplative life. I very much appreciated the articles you have dedicated to this theme. The constitution on women's contemplative life *Vultum Dei Quaerere* of June 29, 2016, and the Instruction *Cor Orans* of April 1, 2018, suppress every form of juridical autonomy and create federations and new bureaucratic organisms as "structures of communion." The obligation to be part of these structures means that monasteries lose *de facto* their autonomy, which is dissolved into an anonymous mass of monasteries that are all moving toward the dissolution of traditional monastic life. The modernist "normalization" of the few monasteries that still resist the revolution would be an inevitable consequence. The juridical suppression of contemplative life we are moving toward does not, however, signify the end of the contemplative spirit, which is becoming ever stronger in response to the secularization of the Church. I know monasteries that have succeeded in securing juridical independence from the Congregation for Religious Life and maintain [authentic] monastic life, supporting the Church in this crisis with their intercessory prayer. I am convinced that, as it once was said, the prayer of the cloisters rules the world.

The sixth anniversary of the election of Pope Bergoglio has passed, even if it felt a bit subdued. One has the impression that even people who once supported him are beginning to distance themselves from him. Is this impression mistaken?

We know that there are forces that want to destroy the Church. Freemasonry is one of these. Yet an open battle against the Church is never productive, because, as Tertullian wrote, the blood of martyrs is the seed of Christians. And this is why, for at least two centuries, a plan has been formulated by anti-Christian forces to conquer the Church from within.

We know that in the 1960s, the Soviet Union and communist regimes of Eastern Europe infiltrated many of their men into the seminaries and Catholic universities. Some of these climbed the ladder and became bishops or even cardinals. But such intentional complicity and activity is not necessary to contribute to the self-destruction of the Church. It is also possible [for Catholics] to become unknowing instruments of someone who manipulates from the outside. In this case, the manipulators chose the most suitable men—those who displayed doctrinal and moral weakness—and influenced them, conditioned them, at times even blackmailed them. The men of the Church are neither infallible nor impeccable, and the Evil One constantly places before them the temptations that the Lord renounced (Mt 4:1–11).

The election of Jorge Mario Bergoglio was directed by a clerical lobby, behind which may be seen the presence of other lobbies or strong powers. I have the impression that the ecclesiastical powers and powers outside the Church that worked for the election of Pope Bergoglio are not satisfied with the results of his pontificate. From their point of view, there have been many words but few practical results. Those who sponsor Pope Francis are ready to abandon him if radical change does not take place. It seems he is being given one last chance to revolutionize the Church in the Amazon Synod this coming October. It seems to me they have already sent signals indicating this.

What signals are you referring to?

[I am referring] to what happened after the summit on pedophilia, which was an obvious failure. The large publications of the international press, from *Corriere della Sera* to *El País*, did not hide their disappointment. It seems to me that the announcement made by the German Bishops' Conference by its president, Cardinal Marx—that they will convoke a local synod that will make binding decisions about sexual morality, priestly celibacy, and the reduction of clerical power—should be understood as an ultimatum. It is the first time that the German bishops have expressed themselves with such clarity. They seem to be saying that if the pope does not cross the Rubicon, they will cross it themselves. In both cases we would find ourselves facing a declared schism.

What consequences would such a separation have?

A declared schism, although evil in itself, could be guided by Divine Providence toward the good. The good that could arise is the awakening of so many people who are asleep, together with the understanding that the crisis did not begin with the pontificate of Pope Francis but has developed for a long time and has deep doctrinal roots. We must have the courage to re-examine what has happened in the last fifty years in the light of the Gospel maxim that a tree is judged by its fruits (Mt 7:16–20). The unity of the Church is a good that should be preserved, but it is not an absolute good. It is not possible to unite what is contradictory, to love truth and falsehood, good and evil, at the same time.

Many Catholics feel discouraged as well as betrayed. Our faith tells us that the forces of evil will not prevail, and yet it is difficult to see a way out of this crisis. Humanly speaking, it seems that everything is collapsing. How will the Church come out of this crisis?

The Church is not afraid of her enemies, and she always wins when Christians fight. On February 4 at Abu Dhabi,

Pope Francis said there is a need of "demilitarizing the heart of man." I believe, on the contrary, that there is a need of militarizing hearts and transforming them into an *Acies Ordinata*, like the one that stood in prayerful protest at Piazza San Silvestro in Rome on February 19 and confirmed the existence of a Catholic resistance against the self-destruction of the Church.[2] There are many other voices of resistance that have made and are making themselves heard.

I believe we must overcome the many misunderstandings that often divide the forces of good people. Instead, we must seek a unity of intention and action among these forces, while maintaining our legitimate different identities. Our adversaries are united in their hatred of the good, and so we ought to be united in our love for the good and for the truth. But we must love a perfect good, a good that is whole and without compromise, because He Who sustains us with His love and power is infinitely perfect. We ought to place all our hope in Him and only in Him. This is why the virtue of hope is the one we ought to cultivate the most, because it makes us strong and perseverant in the battle we are fighting.

2. On February 19, 2019, a hundred Catholics from Italy and abroad lined up in silence in the Piazza San Silvestro in the heart of Rome, in protest of the Vatican's silence on the scandal of homosexuality—the root cause of the clerical sexual abuse crisis in the Church.

Index

Index

Index

Index

Index

Index

About the Author

ROBERTO DE MATTEI is President of the Lepanto Foundation and the founder and director of the Lepanto Cultural Center in Rome. He is the editor of the magazine *Radici Cristiane* as well as the news agency "Corrispondenza Romana." He served as Vice President of the Italian National Research Council from 2003 to 2011. He is the author of numerous books, including *The Second Vatican Council: An Unwritten Story*.

Made in the USA
Monee, IL
03 November 2019